NARRO UGE
AT R
2

Keith Taylorson

PLATEWAY PRESS

ISBN 1 871980 55 0

ISBN 1 871980 55 0

Reprinted 2007

PLATEWAY PRESS
Taverner House, Harling Road, East Harling, Norfolk NR16 2QR

Printed in England by POSTPRINT
Taverner House, Harling Road, East Harling, Norfolk NR16 2QR

Cover and book design by Roy C. Link

Front cover illustration:
Dusk at Sanctuary Wood: a Hunslet 4-6-0T of the 17th ANZAC LROC hauls a trainload of ammunition forward along the Sanctuary Wood line, near Ypres, autumn 1917.
(from an original watercolour painted by Mark Whitmore)

Back cover illustration:
'Paving the way for the Guns'. An engaging portrait of a works train in a rear area location, painted by an unknown artist, based on an 'official' photograph. The locomotive is a 20hp Simplex.
(collection - Keith Taylorson)

Frontispiece:
A Dick Kerr petrol electric loco in use with a Canadian Light Railway Operating Company trundles an ammunition train through the ruined village of Lieven-Angres.
(Canadian 'official')

ACKNOWLEDGEMENTS

I am grateful to Peter Kuntze for providing the German-language Vorwort and to Jacques Pradrayol for the French-language Introduction. Andrew Neale checked the 'locomotive' data quoted throughout the book, and also wrote Chapter 9. The Australian War Memorial kindly provided extracts from the War Diaries and other records of Australian railway units. Thanks are also due to (in alphabetical order): John K. Browning; John Bullen; Paul Cotterell; David Cox; Richard Dunn; Elgin and Moray Libraries; David Gordon Rose; Walter Rothschild; Edoardo Tonarelli; Rodney Weaver.

I am indebted to the Imperial War Museum, London, the Museum of Army Transport, Beverley, and the Australian War Memorial, Canberra, for allowing me access to their photographic archives, and for their generosity in allowing selected photographs to be published here. Other photographic contributors are credited individually, and my grateful thanks go to all these.

CONTENTS

PREFACE

It is nine years since the publication of *"Narrow Gauge at War,"* a largely pictorial survey of the 60cm gauge light railways operated by the British and Dominion armies on the Western Front during World War 1. Production of a second volume has taken longer than anticipated but the result is, hopefully, all the better for it.

In 1987, the only book available on the War Department Light Railways (WDLR) was W J K Davies' *"Light Railways of the First World War."* This scholarly work remains the definitive book on the subject, and it is to be hoped that publication of a second edition will not be too long deferred. Co-incidentally or not, publication of *"Narrow Gauge at War"* presaged a flood of information on the World War 1 light railways, in both book and magazine form. Alfred B Gottwaldt's *"Heeresfeldbahnen"* provides a characteristically thorough analysis of the tactical railways used by the German armies. Richard Dunn's elegiac *"Narrow Gauge to No-Man's Land"* recounts the story of the American armies' 60cm gauge operations. Both these works are the definitive treatises on their subjects, and it is not my role to reprise or refine their conclusions here. But through the courtesy of Richard Dunn, I have been able to quote some further extracts from the history of one US Army unit, the 12th Engineers, whose relationship with the British Army (and thus the WDLR) was probably the closest of all. Finally as far as books are concerned, detailed notes on the achievements of the Canadian Forestry Corps appeared in Cox and Krupa's *"The Kerry Tramway and other Timber Light Railways."*

The last couple of years have seen the publication, in magazine form, of an account of light railway working in the Palestine - Arabia Campaign *(Industrial Railway Record 141),* and an appreciation of the Australian Light Railway Operating Companies has appeared in the *"Bulletin"* of the Australian Railway Historical Society. I have quoted selectively from these accounts, with the kind permission of the respective authors, with a view to making their researches permanently available in book form. Last but far from least I have been greatly privileged, through the good offices of Gordon Wiseman, to be allowed to quote verbatim from the Railway Gazette *"Special War Transportation Number,"* published on September 21 1920. This provides a priceless contemporary analysis of the work of the light railway units, written while the experience of the war was still fresh in people's minds.

The photographic record of the conflict has been enriched by the unearthing of some undiscovered gems, most notably a treasure trove of photographs at the Museum of Army Transport, Beverley. Although to some extent duplicating the Imperial War Museum's archive, this collection contains many 'unknown' views. I am greatly indebted to the Trustees of the Museum, and to the Museum's Railway Adviser, Major J A Robins, for allowing access to this archive, and for agreeing to views from it to be published in this volume.

As in *"Narrow Gauge at War"* I have eschewed a chronological approach to the subject. Instead, I have presented the story of the WDLR in a series of interlinked Chapters, each examining a particular aspect of the light railway organisation or operation. Emphasis has been placed throughout on contemporary or first hand reporting, with the aim of documenting the light railways primarily through the eyes of those who created, maintained or operated them, or of the fighting units that they serviced. My approach assumes the reader's basic appreciation of the background to the creation of the WDLR; totally 'new' readers are recommended to study *"Narrow Gauge at War"* and/or read the brief Introduction provided on the following pages.

Finally I have not attempted to update or supplement the locomotive roster lists published in the first volume, as there is little new or different to add; but thanks to the diligent research of Andrew Neale I am able to present more information on the means by which surplus WDLR locomotives were disposed of when the guns fell silent. I hope that my modest efforts will bring as much pleasure to readers as did *"Narrow Gauge at War,"* and also provide a further tribute to the narrow gauge railway's "finest hour."

Brighton, England, April 1996

INTRODUCTION

Creation of a system of 60cm gauge light railways behind the British, French, German and (later) American front lines during World War 1 was brought about by the changing nature of war itself. Previous European wars were fought by small professional armies, which carried their supplies with them or lived off the land. Most strategists expected the war which erupted in 1914 to follow a similar pattern. But twentieth century technology was to shatter all the carefully laid plans.

By November 1914 the initial rapid German advance through Belgium had been checked at the first battle of Ypres, and in the centre of France the German armies were held, almost at the gates of Paris, by the French at the battle of the Marne. But casualties on all sides were heavy, and the tactical commanders - if, not yet, their High Commands - had come to appreciate the power of the machine gun and the artillery piece. These rendered cavalry obsolete overnight, and could decimate attacking infantry in awesome numbers. Unable to gain ground, both sides dug in, and by the end of 1914 a line of trenches stretched from the channel coast, through Picardy and Champagne, around the fortress at Verdun and on to the Swiss border. For the next 3 years the conflict ebbed and flowed, rarely more than a couple of miles, sometimes only a few yards, either side of this battle line.

Standing armies of millions of men were needed to guard these front lines, and maintain the complex system of communication trenches and logistical support needed to sustain the men at the front. Merely constructing the trenches consumed vast quantities of material - wood for firesteps, trench floors and walls and the construction of dug-outs; sandbags, metal stakes and barbed wire to provide protection. In swampy conditions ferro-concrete might have to be used: in one 2,000 yard section of the front on the La Bassée sector the East Lancashire Regiment used 5,306 bags of cement, 19,384 bags of shingle and 9,692 bags of sand in constructing a single reserve trench line. Even excluding water this comprised 900 tons of material.

World War 1, on the Western Front at least, was primarily a war of artillery. Many soldiers, even those in the front line, never actually saw their enemy. More than 90% of all casualties were caused by artillery fire. Guns of a bewildering size and variety were produced in ever increasing numbers, and deployed in an orgy of destructiveness, reaching a crescendo just before an infantry attack. During the conflict it is calculated that the British armies alone fired off over 170,000,000 rounds of all types - more than five million tons. During the first two weeks of the third Battle of Ypres in

1. A segment of a typical trench system – the quantity of material required is readily apparent. In addition to the front line trenches, reserve and communication trenches also had to be constructed and maintained.
(Author's collection)

2. A British Army lorry typical of the type used during World War 1. Note the solid rubber tyres which wrought havoc with the country roads. (Author's collection)

September 1917, 4,283,550 rounds were fired. Every single round - plus the constant supply of small arms ammunition, grenades, flares etc - had somehow to be conveyed up to the front line.

The costly failure of the British Army's first Somme offensive in July 1916 - caused in part by shortages of key types of ammunition - brought home to the High Command the inadequacy of the supply organisation. While the quantity of supplies needed grew greater the nearer one got to the front line, the problems of supply multiplied. The rural French roads, never designed for military traffic, degenerated into rutted tracks. Thousands of men - diverted from more military roles - toiled to maintain the roads. Beyond the roads lay a nightmare quagmire of pulverised fields, ruined ditches and flooded shell-holes, threaded by temporary duckboard tracks and communication trenches. Through this muddy wasteland every single item needed by the troops - food, water, clothing, medical supplies, tools, timber, barbed wire, mortars, machine guns, rifles, ammunition and yet more ammunition - had to be carried on the backs of men and horses. Thousands of men died as they wandered off the tracks into flooded shell craters, or tripped and fell in the waterlogged trenches and were trampled by the men behind, or were picked off by artillery fire.

The reasons why Britain (alone of the major combatants) had no 'light railway' organisation in place in 1914 may be briefly summarised. Traditionally, when the British Army went to war, it

3. In the struggle to keep supplies moving, the allied armies were obliged to redeploy troops from fighting roles onto the task of road mending. (Author's collection)

4. This trench tramway is constructed by Belgian troops; the early British tramways would have been very similar. (Author's collection)

requisitioned horses from the civilian population. But as the twentieth century dawned, the horse began to be supplanted by the steam engine and (in towns) the electric tramway. Gradually the Army realised it would have to reduce its use of horses too. But what were they to use instead? The creative solution was to encourage the development of standard pieces of machinery that could be requisitioned in time of war, but this idea had one great flaw: anything approved by the Army was not going to sell, because no-one relished having their property confiscated (however pressing the national need). So despite thirty years of experimental work, including trials of pioneering equipment by J B Fell, the British Army had no light railways of their own, or access to any belonging to anyone else. But with lorries shown to be destructive on the roads, and ineffective off them, and horses and manpower unable to deliver the requisite quantities of supplies - especially ammunition - to the front line, something had to be done. The solution, grasped belatedly by the British (the last of the combatants to do so) was the 60cm gauge light railway.

Short lengths of tramway, running on wooden rails, or 'borrowed' track from agricultural tramways, had been used unofficially since 1915. From 1916 onwards their use was officially recognised and, once their usefulness had been proved, massive resources were poured into their construction. The initial War Office programme called for 1,000 miles of 20lb/yd track, 700 steam and 100 petrol locomotives, and 2,800 wagons. Ultimately more than 2,000 miles of track were laid by the British and Dominion Armies. The War Department Light Railways (WDLR) proved their effectiveness during several of the pivotal battles of 1917, and by 1918 were functioning as an indispensable arm of the British Army. Chapter 1 of the following narrative gives a general outline of the organisation which developed - with commendable speed and efficiency - once the need for light railways was proven.

Following the armistice, there was little for the light railways to do, and most were dismantled for scrap. Some sections were absorbed into French agricultural tramways, most notably those in the Froissy - Dompierre region. Many WDLR locomotives - some of which had not even reached the front line - were resold for use on industrial or common carrier railways in Britain and France; their subsequent lives are reasonably well documented. Others enjoyed even more exotic fortunes in countries as far apart as Italy, Spain, Argentina, Australia and India. A few survivors are, even today, thought to be in active service on sugar plantation tramways in India, 80 years after the bloody sacrifice on the Somme that was the genesis for their introduction.

INTRODUCTION

La création d'un systeme de chemin de fer léger à voie de 60 derrière le front, durant la Grande Guerre, a été rendue nécessaire par le caractère nouveau de la guerre elle-même. Les conflits precédéts en Europe ont opposeé des armeés professionnelles, encore relativement petites, ou les combattants transportaient eux-memes leurs approvisionnements - ou bien vivaient de pillages. La plupart des strateèes s'attendaient, en 1914, à ce qu'il en soit de meme dans cette guerre-ci. Mais les technologies du 20ème siècle allaient faire voler en eclats tous les plans soigneusement etablis.

Dès novembre 1914, la rapide avance allemande à travers la Belgique avait été ralentie par la première bataille d'Ypres, et en France les armeés allemandes étaient contenues par les Français, presqu'aux portes de Paris, à la bataille de la Marne. Mais les pertes étaient sévères des deux côtés; et le commandement opérationnel - quoique pas encore le haut-commandement - avait pu se rendre compte du pouvoir destructeur des mitrailleuses et des pièces d'artillerie. De telles armes avaient rendu du jour au lendemain la cavalerie désuète, et étaient capables de faire subir des pertes terribles à l'infanterie lorsque celle-ci passait à l'attaque... Incapables de gagner du terrain, les différentes armées s'enterrèrent, et à la fin de l'anneé 1914 une ligne continue de trancheés s'étendait depuis la Manche, à travers la Picardie et la Champagne, entourant la forteresse de Verdun puis couronnant les Vosges, et jusqu'à la frontiere suisse. Durant les trois ans et demi qui suivirent, les hostilites concemerent rarement plus de quelques kilomètres autour de cette ligne de front, et quelquefois même seulement quelques mètres.

Des millions d'hommes étaient nécessaires pour monter la garde sur ce front quasi immobile, et entretenir le système compliqué de boyaux de communication et de support logistique permettant l'approvisionnement des combattants. La seule construction des tranchées consommait de grandes quantités de matériel: bois pour les postes de tir, les murs et le plancher des tranchees, la construction des abris et des caches souterraines; sacs de sable, pieux métalliques et fil de fer barbelé pour créer des obstacles. Dans certains environnements humides, il etait indispensable de bétonner; ainsi, sur 2km de front du cote de La Bassée, le Regiment de l'East Lancashire utilisa 5306 sacs de ciment, 19384 sacs de galets, et 9692 sacs de sable, pour etablir une ligne de tranchees de reserve... Eau exclue, cela representait 900 tonnes d'approvisionnements!

Le côteux échec de la première offensive de l'armée britannique sur la Somme, en juillet 1916, - échec du en partie a la difficulté d'acheminer certains types de munitions en quantité suffisante -, attira l'attention du haut-commandement sur l'inadaptation du systeme d'approvisionnement. Plus

5. Unlike the British, the French Army had invested much effort into construction of a system of 60cm gauge tactical railways. Lengthy systems served the frontier forts at Verdun, Epinal and Toul. This view is believed to be taken at Verdun pre-war, and depicts a train hauled by two Pechôt-Bourdon twin locos (only one of which is visible) conveying a visiting British mission. (Plateway Press)

6. **Considerable devastation was caused by the first German attacks. In addition, the retreating Allied armies destroyed bridges to slow down the enemy's advance.**
(Author's collection)

on s'approchait du front, plus les volumes necessaires s'accroissaient et plus les difficultes de transport se multipliaient. Les chemins ruraux français, non conçus bien sûr pour un trafic militaire, se transformaient en pistes pleines d'ornières. Des milliers d'hommes, soustraits a leurs taches militaires, peinaient à entretenir les routes. Au-delà de celles-ci, c'était un paysage cauchemardesque de fondrières, de champs réduits en miettes, de fossés en ruines et de trous d'obus noyés, parmi lesquels se faufilaient des pistes en caillebotis et des tranchées de communication. Tout ce qui etait necessaire a la vie des troupes de premiere ligne devait franchir ces étendues fangeuses: la nourriture, l'eau potable, les vêtements, les fournitures médicales, les outils, le bois, les rouleaux de barbelé, les mortiers de tranchée, les mitrailleuses, les fusils, les munitions, et toujours davantage de munitions... Tout cela devait être apporté à dos d'homme et de mulet, et généralement de nuit. Des milliers d'hommes périrent à cette tâche; ils s'égaraient hors de la piste et tombaient dans des cratères remplis d'eau, glissaient dans les boyaux et étaient piétinés par ceux qui les suivaient, ou encore subissaient des bombardements d'artillerie. Quelque chose devait être fait, et les Anglais, suivant enfin l'exemple des autres belligérants, adoptèrent "officiellement" le chemin de fer a voie de 60.

7. **This view of the Somme battlefield early in July 1916 graphically illustrates the effect that massed artillery had on the landscape.**
(Author's collection)

8. Further back from the front line, French troops are depicted being resupplied with ammunition by one of their 60cm gauge systems. The wagons are very similar to the WDLR 'D' class. (Author's collection)

Depuis 1915, certaines unites utilisaient déjà, de leur propre autorité, de courtes longueurs de rails ou de barres métalliques, fixées sur des morceaux de bois transversaux; c'etaient parfois des rails portables, emprruntes à des chemins de fer agricoles. A partir de 1916, l'usage de tels matériels fut reconnu officiellement et encouragé. Après que leur utilité ait été clairement démontréé, des ressources massives furent affectées à leur construction. Le premier programme du "War Office" en ce domaine comportait une commande de 1600km (1000 miles) de voie en rails de 10 kg par metre (20 livres par yard), 700 locomotives a vapeur, 100 tracteurs a moteur thermique, et 2800 wagons. En tout, plus de 3000km de voie furent établis par les armees de Grande-Bretagne et des Dominions.

Les chemins de fer légers du War Department (WDLR, War Department Light Railways) prouverent leur efficacité durant plusieurs des batailles majeures de 1917, et en 1918 ils etaient considérés comme une part indispensable de l'armée britannique.

Après l'armistice, certains materiels de ces réseaux et même certaines lignes servirent à l'évacuation des deblais et à la reconstruction des régions du nord-est de la France dévastées par le conflit. Mais, rapidement, la plupart des locomotives, wagons, et rails, furent ferraillés et disparurent jusque dans la mémoire collective, car le public eut tendance à idéaliser le rôle pourtant modeste des véhicules routiers, dans les hostilites. Certaines des lignes temporairement conservees pour la reconstruction, de 1919 à 1924 environ, passérent ensuite sous le contrôle de sucreries pour devenir des réseaux agricoles; ainsi autour de Froissy et de Dompierre, en Picardie. Beaucoup de locomotives du WDLR, dont certaines n'avaient même pas eu le temps d'atteindre les réseaux du front, furent vendues par l'Etat à des chemins de fer industriels ou secondaires. D'autres connurent un sort plus exotique, dans des pays tels l'Italie, l'Espagne, l'Argentine, l'Australie, ou l'Inde. Hormis les rares modèles préservés dans des musées, quelques surivantes sont encore en service actif sur des réseaux sucriers des Indes, 80 années apres les sanglants évènements de la Somme qui avaient été à l'origine de leur construction.

9. A British heavy gun in action. Supplying such guns with ammunition became the prime task of the light railways on all sides.
(Author's collection)

VORWORT

Der Erste Weltkrieg entwickelte sich ganz anders als die Strategen in den Generalstäben vorher geplant hatten. Die Planer waren vom klassischen Konzept des Bewegungskrieges ausgegangen, in dem kleine bewegliche Einheiten in das feindliche Gebiet vorstoßen sollten. Diese Einheiten sollten ihren Nachschub mit sich führen oder im Notfall auch unterwegs requirieren.

Niemand hatte aber damit gerechnet, daß sich der Krieg zum Stellungskrieg entwickeln könnte. Dieser Fall trat aber ein, als im November 1914 der Schlieffen- Plan scheiterte. Kaiser Wilhelms Generalstab hatte geplant, durch belgisches Gebiet vorzustoßen und Paris durch eine Zangenbewegung zu umfassen. Die Alliierten brachten den deutschen Vormarsch im Norden in der ersten Schlacht von Ypern zum Stehen, und im Süden gelang es den Franzosen, den direkten Vormarsch auf Paris in der Marneschlacht zu unterbinden. Was sich hier fast so harmlos wie ein Sportbericht anhört, war ein blutiges Gemetzel, das auf beiden Seiten Zehntausende von Toten und Verwundeten kostete. Maschinengewehre und neuzeitliche Artillerie machten die Infanterie und Kavallerie völlig hilflos und schutzlos. Die berittenen Truppen mußten abgezogen werden, und die Infanterie konnte sich nur noch verschanzen.

10. Through 1915 and 1916 the only methods approved by the British for transporting ammunition up to the front line were men and horses. The low carrying capacity of the latter will be noted.
(Author's collection)

Ende des Jahres 1914 hatte sich eine feste Frontlinie entwickelt, die sich von der belgischen Nordseeküste durch die Champagne und Lothringen bis zur Schweizer Grenze bei Basel hinzog. Wiederholte Vorstöße der Deutschen wie auch der Alliierten blieben erfolglos. Auch in blutigen Materialschlachten gelang es beiden Seiten nicht, jeweils mehr als zwei oder drei Kilometer weit in das gegnerische Gebiet vorzustoßen. Oft genug wurden ganze Regimenter verheizt, um nur 100 oder 150 m weit vorzustoßen.

Millionen von Soldaten waren notig, um die Schützengräben und Feldbefestigungen anzulegen und instandzuhalten, um den umfangreichen Nachschub heranzuschaffen und um die Verwundeten zu bergen. Beim Bau von Schützengräben und Unterstanden mußte der Erdaushub abgefahren werden und Tausende von Tonnen Holz für den Ausbau der Gräben und Unterstände mußten antransportiert werden. Für die Feldbefestigungen mußten Sandsäcke, Wellblech, Zaunpfähle und Stacheldraht an die Front transportiert werden. Vereinzelt wurde auch schon Beton für den Befestigungsbau verwendet, zum Beispiel in sumpfigem Gelände oder bei besonders starkem Beschuß. Bei La Bassee zum Beispiel mußte ein Schützengraben in der zweiten Linie durch ein Moor gelegt werden, und für knapp 2km Graben wurden hier über 900 t Sand, Kies und Zement verbraucht, die nur unter größter Mühe an die Baustellen gebracht werden konnten.

Der gesamte Verkehr wickelte sich anfangs auf der Straße ab. Die Landstraßen und Feldwege waren diesen Anforderungen nicht gewachsen und wurden durch die Fuhrwerke und primitiven Lastkraftwagen bald völlig zerstört. Zehntausende von Mann mußten beim Straßenbau eingesetzt werden, sie konnten aber nur die schlimmsten Schäden beseitigen. Im unmittelbaren Frontgebiet schließlich kam man mit Fahrzeugen überhaupt nicht mehr weiter. Hier mußten Trägerkolonnen eingesetzt werden, die in ständiger Lebensgefahr den Nachschub durch die Verbindungsgräben und die grundlosen Granattrichter an die Front bringen mußten. Die Deutschen und die Franzosen zogen schon früh die Konsequenzen aus diesen unhaltbaren Verhältnissen und begannen mit dem Einsatz von Feldbahnen. Die Franzosen griffen dabei auf die *chemins de fer Decauville* ihrer Festungsartillerie zurück und die Deutschen auf das Schmalspurmaterial der preußischen Eisenbahn- Brigaden.

Die Engländer zögerten noch lange. Das Londoner Kriegsministerium lehnte offiziell den Einsatz von Schmalspurbahnen ab mit dem kategorischen Satz von General Lord Kitchener: "*That is not our way of working!*". Untergeordnete Stellen dachten aber anders. Ende 1915 hatten die englischen

11. A trench tramway built by Belgian troops, typical of those used by all armies in the conflict. The professionally constructed bridge is of interest.
(Author's collection)

12. The German armies were thoroughly prepared for the demands of a modern war. Their 'Feldbahns' were laid in the wake of the German advance, and sections of French light railway were also taken over. In this view, fresh troops move up to the line near Menin. (Eisenbahnarchiv)

Truppen schon erste provisorische Bahnen angelegt mit Gleismaterial und Wagen von landwirtschaftlichen Bahnen oder aus französischen Bestanden. Vereinzelt wurden sogar selbst hergestellte Schienen aus Holz verwendet! Anfang 1916 gelang es dann den Praktikem von der Front schlieBlich, das Kriegsministerium umzustimmen, und London leitete ein umfangreiches Beschaffungsprogramm fur Fe!dbahnen ein. Die erste Beschaffungsstufe umfaßte rund 1600km vormontierte Gleisjoche, 700 Dampfloks, 100 Verbrennungsmotorloks und 2800 Wagen. Gegen Ende des Krieges hatten dann die englischen Truppen und ihre kanadischen, australischen und südafrikanischen Verbündeten ein Netz von fast 3500km Gleislänge in Betrieb.

Die erhebliche strategische Bedeutung der schmalspurigen Bahnen stellte sich im Verlauf der großen Schlachten von 1917 heraus, und 1918 war ihre Bedeutung als unentbehrlicher Eckpfeiler des Nachschubsystems allgemein anerkannt. Aber bald schon war es vorbei mit ihnen, denn nach dem Waffenstillstand im November 1918 wurden die Bahnen überflüssig. Die meisten Strecken wurden abgebaut und Fahrzeuge und Gleismaterial an Händler verkauft. Die Händler verkauften das Bahnmaterial weiter an Kunden in aller Welt von Argentinien bis hin nach Indien und Australien. Einige wenige Fahrzeuge sind heute noch auf Plantagenbahnen in Indien im Einsatz. Ein geringer Teil der Bahnstrecken blieb auch nach 1918 noch in Betrieb, und zwar zunächst für die fianzösische Wiederaufbauverwaltung *"Regie des Zones Liberées"* und teilweise auch im Besitz von Ziegeleien, Zuckerfabriken und ähnlichen Untemehmen. Die heutige Museumsbahn Froissy- Cappy- Dompierre ist zum Beispiel eine ehemalige englische Militärbahn, und viele Eisenbahnfreunde sind sich kau n bewußt, welchen grausigen Ursprung diese ländliche Schmalspur- Idylle hat!

THE WESTERN FRONT 1918

Chapter One

LIGHT RAILWAY WORKING ON THE WESTERN FRONT

An account of the Construction and Operation of Light Railways in France, and a Description of the Plant and Equipment.

from the 'Railway Gazette' Special War Transportation Number, September 21, 1920. Reprinted by courtesy of Railway Gazette International.

THE IMPORTANCE OF THE PART PLAYED BY RAILWAYS in modern warfare has for long been realised by the high commands of all nations, and the excellence of the work performed by the standard gauge lines on all fronts during the great war is pretty generally recognised. Of the work of the light railways of 60cm gauge, however, little is generally known. This may be attributed partly to the fact that their work differed so vastly from anything met with in peacetime operation, and partly to the veil of secrecy which naturally hid their operations from public notice. Without doubt, the most striking feature of the campaign on the Western front, so far as transportation interests are concerned, was the importance of the part played by the 60cm lines in the transport of material and personnel in the zone lying between the standard gauge railheads and the infantry and artillery positions, and the story of their operation is full of interest to the student of transportation.

Establishment of a Directorate of Light Railways

The home depot of the Royal Engineers' railway troops has, for many years, been situated at Longmoor Camp, Hants, which is reached from Bordon Station, on the London & South Western Railway, by a short standard gauge military line. In pre-war days the railway branch of the Royal Engineers consisted simply of two companies of men - the 8th and the 10th - and was therefore quite a small branch of that famous corps. Naturally, on the outbreak of war, these two companies were totally unable to cope with the working of the military railways at home and overseas, and so

13. The first British railway troops deployed in France in late 1914 were engaged in working sections of the French railways. They were known as the Railway Operating Division (ROD). Later, the ROD units were to form the nucleus of the Light Railway Operating Companies. In this view near St. Omer, two Royal Engineers pose with ROD No. 6, a Beyer Peacock 4-6-4T built for Netherlands Railways but commandeered by the War Dept. for use in France.
(Author's collection)

it came about that the various railway companies in the United Kingdom and in all corners of the Empire were asked to supply trained personnel to form new units.

These new units were, so far as the Western front is concerned, really composed of construction troops, with a sprinkling of operating and locomotive men, and it was not until the spring of 1915 that the Railway Operating Division was formed to operate sections of French standard gauge line given over to the British authorities and such new standard gauge lines as had been laid by us in France. About February, 1916, the Railway Operating Division, in addition to its work on the standard gauge, began to operate certain narrow gauge lines taken over from the French, but towards the close of 1916, with the growth of the narrow gauge system, the Directorate of Light Railways came into being, and numbers of men were then transferred from the Railway Operating Division, where they had been engaged on both standard and narrow gauge working, to the Light Railway Directorate. With the light railway lines which had been taken over from the French authorities, and others which were gradually constructed, there became a regular network of narrow gauge railways behind the whole of the Western front operated entirely by the Directorate of Light Railways, leaving to the Railway Operating Division the operating of the standard gauge alone.

Organisation of Light Railway Working

The light railway organisation in France was briefly as follows. Under the General Officer Commanding-in-Chief of the British Army came the Director-General of Transportation, to whom the

14. An early light railway used during the campaign to take High Wood, on the Somme, in July – October 1916. A train hauled by two unidentified 20hp Simplexes transports a mixed group of Gordon Highlanders and Durham Light Infantry. No less than 35 soldiers are accommodated on 3 Hudson skips and a 4-wheel open wagon, plus the locos.
(Imperial War Museum, Q4387)

15. An improvised train consisting of two home built 4-wheel flat wagons, utilising commercial wheel sets and axle boxes, behind a Simplex 20hp tractor, is conveying track panels. These are light enough to be lifted by two men and can be laid flat on the ground with minimal preparation.
(Imperial War Museum, Q4381)

Director of Light Railways at General Headquarters was directly responsible. For each army there was an Assistant Director of Light Railways and under him a Superintendent of Light Railways. Then came the Army Traffic Superintendent, the Locomotive and Tractor[1] Superintendents, the various commanding officers of operating companies and the district traffic, Locomotive and Tractor Superintendents. Each army also had a chief train controller, and numerous other officers such as an officer in charge of statistics and a stores officer. The organisation thus worked out on the following lines: -

G.O.C.-in-C.
Director-General of Transportation
Director of Light Railways
Assistant Directors of Light Railways
Superintendents of Light Railways

- Army Traffic Superintendents
  District Traffic Superintendents
- Army Locomotive Superintendents
  District Locomotive Superintendents
- Army Tractor Superintendents
  District Tractor Superintendents
- O.Cs. Operating Companies
  Statistical and Miscellaneous Officers

It frequently happened that an operating company would be split up into two or three detachments situated at various points with an officer in charge of each detachment, all nominally under the commanding officer of the company, but in practice left almost entirely to their own devices. Each army corps also had a corps light railway officer attached to it, who acted as a kind of liaison officer between corps and the light railways.

The gauge of the light railway was 60cm - approximately 2ft - and for hauling trains steam, petrol and petrol-electric locomotives were utilised. In the rear areas steam locomotives were largely but not exclusively used; in the forward areas these were invariably replaced by petrol and petrol-electric tractors. Owing to the absence of escaping smoke, steam and sparks, the two latter types of locomotives were particularly suitable for work in the forward zones, where to have run a steam locomotive would have meant instant detection by the enemy and the consequent drawing of hostile fire.

Types of Steam Locomotives Employed

The principal types of steam locomotives in use on the light railways were as follows, Hunslet 4-6-0T, Hudson 0-6-0T, Baldwin 4-6-0T, Barclay 0-6-0T and American 2-6-2T. All these locomotives performed excellent work, and as the details may be of interest they will be found tabulated below.

	Hudson 0-6-0 Well Tank	Hunslet 4-6-0 Side Tank	Baldwin 4-6-0 Side Tank	Barclay 0-6-0 Well Tank	American 2-6-2 Side Tank
Cylinder diameter	6½in	9½in	9in	6¾in	9in
Stroke	12in	12in	12in	10¾in	14in
Length of boiler	5ft 6in	5ft	7ft	5ft 10in	-
Diameter of boiler	2ft 1in	2ft 9in	2ft 9in	2ft 2¾in	2ft 8in
Dia. of bogie wheels	-	1ft 6½in	1ft 4in	-	1ft 4in
Dia. of coupled wheels	1ft 11in	2ft	1ft 11½in	1ft 10in	2ft 3in
Coupled wheelbase	4ft 2in	5ft 6in	5ft 10in	4ft 4in	5ft 6in
Total wheelbase	4ft 2in	13ft	12ft 4in	4ft 4in	15ft 9in
Heating Surface (Sq.ft)					
Tubes	108·5	168	231	111	-
Firebox	17·5	37	23·5	20	-
Total	126	205	254·5	131	272
Grate area	3·25	3·95	5·6	3·5	5·5
Capacity of tank (galls.)	110	375	396	110	396
Capacity of Bunkers (cwt.)	3·5	15	15·7	3·5	15
Working pressure					
Lb.per Sq. in	150	160	178	160	175
Tractive force (lbs.)	2,790	5,415 (at 75% b.p.)	5,510	-	-
Valve gear	Walschaert	Walschaert	Walschaert	Walschaert	Walschaert
Brake	Hand	Steam & hand	Steam & hand	Hand	Steam & hand
Firebox - material	Copper	Copper	Copper	Copper	Copper
Tubes - material & No.	Steel - 45	Brass - 86	Brass - 83	Brass - 45	Brass - 54
Width overall	5ft 8in	6ft 3½in	6ft 11in	5ft 5¼in	6ft 9in
Height overall	8ft 8¾in	8ft 11½in	9ft 3¼in	8ft 4¼in	9ft
Length over couplers	15ft 5¼in	19ft 10¾in	19ft 6⅛in	14ft 2⅞in	-
Weight - in tons					
Empty	5·775	10·9	11·04	5·9	-
In working order	6·8875	14·05	14·7	7·0	-
Max. weight - in tons					
On a pair of wheels	2·3875	3·5	3·46	-	3·5
Per ft run of wheelbase	1·653	1·08	1·14	-	-
Per ft run over couplers	0·446	0·708	-	-	-
On coupled wheels	6·887	10·5	10·38	-	-

16. In practice, the track panels, if left unsupported, sank into soft ground and would be unsuitable for locomotive working. Wooden sleepers are therefore inserted at intervals to provide a firmer foundation. (Museum of Army Transport)

17. The first steam locomotive type despatched to the British forces for use in France was the 'Hudson' 0-6-0WT. Based ironically on a German design, the locos were actually built by Hudswell Clarke. No. 102, pictured here at Fricourt with two early 'C' class wagons, was ex-works in May 1916. Note the absence of any insignia identifying her as a British Army locomotive. (Imperial War Museum, Q4344)

18. As their contribution to the war effort, Andrew Barclay built 25 of a modified version of their 'F' class 0-6-0WT. They were ordered in August 1916, as Hudswell Clarke could not produce their order fast enough. This cheerful scene appears to be taken after the end of hostilities; a minor mystery is the '1009' number plate, the locos originally being numbered 601-625, but whether 1009 was formerly 609 is unknown. (Collection – Jim Peden)

Petrol and Petrol-Electric Locomotives

The working of the petrol and petrol-electric locomotives in the forward zones forms a particularly interesting study, for the conditions there were naturally not of the best, and the demands made upon the locomotives as heavy as they very well could be. Until something like 15 years ago little attention had been paid by British engineers to the possibilities of petrol locomotives for commercial haulage. This may be attributed to the fact that there was already on the market a German-made petrol locomotive selling at such a low figure as to make it difficult for British makers to compete with it in the open market. There was no question of any superiority of design or high-class of manufacture. The working results of the German product were, however, such as to preclude our engineers seriously attempting to compete with it. The petrol locomotive, too, was looked upon by most engineers, to all intents and purposes, as an unknown quantity, and locomotive engineers preferred to devote their attention solely to the production of, and improvements to, the steam locomotive, in the manufacture of which engine British makers have attained such world-wide renown.

A few British firms did, however, about this time seriously begin to study the possibilities of petrol traction on rails, and as a result of many years of time, study and usage, the petrol locomotive has gradually grown to be the efficient engine it is to-day. Faults there naturally were in their early efforts, but thanks to the indomitable perseverance of the British manufacturers these were eventually overcome, and to-day the British petrol locomotive is a perfect engine, far ahead of its

19. For 'line' work, larger locomotives were needed. The Hunslet Engine Co., Leeds, offered a neat and powerful 4-6-0T, reminiscent of contemporary 'colonial' design. No. 311 was one of the initial batch, ex-works between 10 August 1916 and 15 August 1916, and is pictured with two Baldwin 4-6-0T's in the background.
(Collection – R T Horne)

German competitor. Its introduction has placed a new means of haulage - speedy, reliable and economical - at our command.

The war was responsible for enormous improvements in this form of traction, just as it was for a hundred-and-one other valuable developments in the engineering world, and no branch of our engineering industry was quicker to respond to the demands made upon it than that of the petrol engine manufacturers. Large quantities of petrol locomotives were called for by the War Office, having for their special task the hauling of the heavy ammunition trains on the light railways to the guns. So successful did these locomotives become in this direction that one great manufactory[3] quickly increased its output to something like 30 times its pre-war turn-out in order to meet the phenomenal demand for its products. When one considers the severe conditions under which these petrol locomotives had to work, and the fact that the greater proportion of their army drivers were hurriedly trained and possessed little or no previous experience of this class of engine, or, in fact, of engines of any description, the wonderful results attained are little short of marvellous.

20. British builders were not able to mass produce locomotives in the quantities now needed by the WDLR. The Baldwin Locomotive Co. came to the rescue with an existing design, their class 10-12-D, already produced for the French military railways in Morocco. Almost 500 were built for the WDLR between October 1916 and April 1917.
(Lens of Sutton)

Utility of the Petrol Locomotive

Many of the narrow gauge railways in France were originally laid for horse traction and man haulage, hence it was essential that the weight of the locomotives, particularly those which were intended for service in the forward areas, should be kept within reasonable figures, and provision was therefore made by the makers of petrol locomotives for war service to increase or reduce their adhesion by removable ballast weights, thus providing for the locomotive a much wider sphere of operation. One of the fundamental principles covering the design of the locomotives was that, while being comparatively simple to control, they should, in addition, be capable of withstanding a very considerable amount of rough usage and overloading.

The light railway lines on the Western front were often, of necessity, laid without due regard to symmetry or rigidity. These conditions alone were obviously not helpful towards the locomotives operating at their best. In the winter months the rails were frequently submerged in snow, water and mud, and truth to tell, many suffered rough treatment at the hands of inexperienced drivers. Human nature being what it is many of the locomotives were almost inevitably driven through shelled areas at considerably above the speed for which they were designed, and this although speaking volumes for their capabilities in an emergency, was bound in time to impair the efficiency of any engine. Notwithstanding these adverse conditions, the petrol locomotive came out of the campaign with an established reputation.

The principal types of petrol locomotives used on the Western front were the 20 and 40hp "Simplex" petrol locomotives manufactured by the Motor Rail & Tramcar Company, Limited, Bedford, and the 40hp petrol-electric locomotives manufactured by the British Westinghouse Company, Limited, and Dick, Kerr & Co., Limited. All of these performed excellent work and gave complete satisfaction.

21. New locomotives for the WDLR were shipped on standard gauge flat cars via the French or Belgian railways to a convenient transhipment point. A ramp of sleepers, as shown here, allows the ng loco to be safely lowered down to ground level. Two Baldwin 4-6-0T's, one of which is No. 1096, are being delivered, early in 1917.
(Museum of Army Transport)

22. Even the mighty Baldwins were unable to meet the WDLR's increasing demands as the light railways expanded in 1917. The Alco (Cooke) Locomotive Works therefore supplied a batch of 100 2-6-2T's which were allocated to British and Australian units. The 2-6-2T wheel arrangement was more suited to front line conditions, with the inevitable amount of bunker first working.
(Lens of Sutton)

The Simplex Petrol Locomotive

These petrol locomotives were used in greater numbers than any other types of tractor, and were constantly to be seen hauling long trains in the forward zones, and frequently also in the rear areas. The machinery of both locomotives as a whole is carried upon two pairs of wheels and axles, both of which are driven from the engine. The prime mover consists of an internal combustion engine, which may be of either two, four or more[4] cylinders, and is similar in many respects to that adopted in the construction of heavy commercial motor lorries.

The engine is placed across the centre of the frame, and is fitted with an extra large flywheel carrying a specially-designed friction clutch. The clutch is directly coupled to the driving shaft in the gearbox, and from this power is taken to operate the locomotive. Upon the locomotive frame are mounted the necessary fuel tank, radiator and silencer, and the radiator is kept cool by means of a fan driven from the engine. Sanding gear is also provided, with the necessary foot pedals. The wheelbase is remarkably short, and the centre of gravity low, thus permitting of the roughest track and the sharpest gradient being safely negotiated.

23. Workhorse of the WDLR was the 20hp Simplex, delivered in large numbers between February 1916 and January 1918. Able to operate on the lightest track, the Simplex's main drawback was the lack of protection – even from the weather – for the driver. The first few batches were numbered in the series 200-299. Deliveries from 23 December 1916 used the 'LR' prefix: LR2608 is one of a batch ordered on 1st January 1918.
(Lens of Sutton)

24. Motor Rail also designed a 40hp petrol loco specially for WDLR conditions, and built them in three variants, 'open', 'protected' and 'armoured'. Illustrated is a 'protected' example, with curved end sheets of heavy gauge steel providing the driver with basic protection. No. 3022 was one of the final batch, ex-works between July and December 1918, and one of the last locos to be delivered to the WDLR.
(Lens of Sutton)

Three types of the 40hp "Simplex" petrol locomotive were used on the Western front - the open, protected and armoured types. The first type did not give the driver great protection from shell fragments and shrapnel but the two other types provided considerable protection, and this protective armour was the means of saving the life of more than one driver in France.

25. An example of the 'armoured' Simplex; closed up, it would protect the crew against anything but a direct hit from shellfire. Note the exhaust positioned on the roof, and the observation slits in the bodywork. Conditions inside the shut down loco were, however, hardly bearable, and only 27 were built.
(Lens of Sutton)

26. The final WDLR class, 40hp petrol electrics from Dick Kerr and British Westinghouse (who built 100 each) were originally designed to run cab-to-cab, thus the rear centre door shown to good advantage here. The PE's found especial favour with Canadian Light Rly Operating Companies, who are using this Dick Kerr example to haul their distinctive inspection car, built in their own yards at Lens. (Canadian 'official,' CO3566)

Light Railway Rolling-Stock

Almost the whole of the rolling-stock in use on the light railways on the Western front was specially built by English wagon makers to the order of the War Office, and the total stock of trucks of all types in use numbered many thousands. The wagons were all of substantial construction, with, in many cases, pressed-steel underframes, bogie trucks predominating. The types of wagons in most frequent use were the open bogie trucks of from 12 to 17ft inside length, and the open box wagons with an inside length of 6 and 8ft respectively. Another useful type of truck was a well-wagon fitted with detachable iron stanchions for the transport of ammunition, rails, timber &c. The trucks had an inside length of 17ft 8in, with a well 7ft 4in in length and 1ft 7in deep. Bogie tank wagons, having a capacity of 1,600 galls., were also used extensively for the transport of drinking water to the artillery and infantry. A smaller type of tank wagon was also utilised for journeys on very exposed routes. Special types of open and covered trucks were also used for the transport of wounded from the battlefield, as break-down vans, and on the tractor repair trains. Steel tip trucks were also extensively made use of for construction work, train loads of 20 or 80 of these cars loaded with ballast being a common sight in all the army areas. There were also numerous odd types of wagon, many built overseas, for special purposes, such as inspection cars, ration wagons and the like. The First Army possessed a most attractive covered inspection car lettered outside "F.A.L.R" (First Army Light Railways), and many notable passengers travelled on inspection trips over the light railways in that army area in this comfortable coach.

Above: 27. The Crewe Tractor was based on the Ford Model T, and was intended for both road and rail use. Its poor load hauling capacity limited its use to working on the trench tramways, as in this view showing No. 39 hauling shells for the 9th Regiment, 'A' battery, Royal Garrison Artillery, during the battle of Langemarck on 19 August 1917.
(Imperial War Museum, Q2661)

Below: 28. One of the light railways' chief functions was transport of material for constructing and maintaining trenches. This train hauled by Baldwin 4-6-0T No. 737 conveys duckboards (for flooring), vertical trusses for reinforcing the trench sides, and sandbags for 'topping out'. The troops are Pioneers of the 17th (Service) Battalion, Northumberland Fusiliers, and their full combat gear shows they are in a forward area.
(Museum of Army Transport)

29. A view of Westenhoek goods yard in Belgium. This gives an idea of the sheer scale of the WDLR's traffic as the light railways built up their ton/mileage. Most traffic in this view appears to consist of boxed rifle ammunition.
(Museum of Army Transport)

High speeds were naturally impossible on the narrow gauge lines and 10mph was considered a good running speed for loaded trains over most lines. On good stretches of track, however, speeds of 15 and even 20mph were not uncommonly attained. Train loads varied very considerably, according to circumstances, but there was rarely more than 150 tons behind the locomotive. Wagon loads would be anything from 1 to 10 tons, according to the type of wagon utilised and the nature of the traffic. Ammunition naturally provided the best loads.

Method of Working Trains

Time-tables were practically non-existent on the narrow-gauge lines, except for special large troop movements, trains simply running as and when required. The "rush" hours for traffic were usually from 6 p.m. to 6 a.m., or thereabouts. The running of trains was controlled entirely by telephone, and there were no fixed signals on the line. Any number of trains could travel in the same direction from one telephone post to another at the same time, the only stipulation being that sufficient distance was maintained between the engine of the second train and the rear wagon of the first to permit of the second pulling up clear of the preceding one if necessary. In the forward area at busy times there was one almost continuous string of trains travelling through the section at the same time.

The train crew consisted of a locomotive driver, fireman and guard, although on trains drawn by petrol locomotives the fireman was dispensed with. There was no guard's brake van on the train, the guard riding in between the last wagon and the last wagon but one, from which position he manipulated the wagon brakes as necessary, this frequently entailing him working his way along the train as it was in motion. On several light railway wagons captured from the enemy we found small hinged seats of wood about 1ft square fixed on to either end of the truck for the use of the guard. As, however, the guard was constantly on and off the train at control posts and sidings, and journeys of more than an hour's duration were not frequent, we did not consider any useful purpose would be served by adopting a similar arrangement, especially as it would have meant foreshortening the wagon in order to provide room for the seat.

Headlights were carried on the locomotives after dark, and usually a tail lamp on the last wagon of the train, except in the forward area, where, owing to the danger of drawing enemy fire, head and tail lamps were in many cases replaced by luminous discs, which could not be distinguished at any considerable distance. On very exposed portions of the line no lights whatever were carried, and there was no daylight working on these branches, whilst occasionally the lines were camouflaged with cloth covers during the daytime. The greater part of the track was single line, with passing places at each telephone box or control post. All behind the front was one vast network of light railway lines, so that if one section of line happened to be blown out by enemy shell fire, it was often possible to divert traffic to another route for the time being. The whole system of traffic working was naturally very free and easy, and much latitude was allowed officers and men in working. Difficulties were constantly cropping up, especially in night working in the forward areas, where, for instance, it was no unusual thing to have three or four derailments in one section in one night, and it was usually the "man on the spot" who had to decide how the difficulty should be overcome.

Extension of Light Railway System

For the first three years or so of war, the light railways simply covered the district from the front to about 10 miles behind, but as time went on the desirability of having lines of light railway leading back for, say, 20 miles became evident. Particularly was this noticed after the German advance towards Amiens in the spring of 1918. Many locomotives and tractors, together with much rolling

30. This posed view shows the technique of rerailing a locomotive using two cranes. Derailments were frequent, due to the state of the track, damage by enemy artillery fire, or sometimes the instability of the locomotives themselves (see "Narrow Gauge at War", illustrations 37 and 38). A rerailing operation like this would be highly visible to enemy observers and would be unlikely to be carried out for real, in daytime at any rate, in range of the German artillery!
(Museum of Army Transport)

31. Another demonstration of lifting power: a single mobile crane is sufficient to lift an 'open' 40hp Simplex. A partly constructed locomotive shed is behind the crane, and two Alco 2-6-2T's can be seen in the background.
(Imperial War Museum, Q35477)

stock, then fell into the hands of the enemy - who also worked with a 60cm gauge - which might have been saved had we possessed one single line of light railway track leading far enough back from the front. As it was, locomotives and rolling-stock were in several cases brought as far as the terminus of the light railways, and there abandoned or destroyed, owing to the inability of the standard gauge to get them away in time. After this, lines of escape to the back areas were constructed at suitable points.

Workshops

Extensive workshops were provided at Berguette for light railway work, and also for attending to the steam rollers and lorries working on the roads. In addition to these main workshops for erection and heavy work, repair trains were provided to facilitate the carrying out of light repairs in the army areas.

At the end of 1917, all the store depots were concentrated in the northern areas, the reason for this being that as transportation material was imported via Dunkirk, this gave a shorter rail-haul from the port, and, additionally, the railway workshops were established in the north. Following the enemy offensive early in 1918, and his advance towards Hazebrouck, No. 2 depot (Berguette), No. 3 depot (Aire), and No. 4 depot (Borre) had to be evacuated, this being effected with practically no loss of material. No. 2 was moved first to Zeneghem and then to Beaurainville, No. 3 first to Zeneghem, then to Richborough and afterwards back to Aire, and No. 4 to Audruicq.

Following the evacuation, new depots were promptly commenced at Beaurainville, to which place the light railway workshops had been removed, and at Lory, south of the Seine. Both depots were designed to hold track and general stores of all kinds in order to avoid having everything concentrated in one area. At the same time, the D.G.M.R. arranged to hold the main reserve of general stores and tractor spare parts at Purfleet and the reserve of I.W.T.[5] material at Richborough. The forward locomotive shops at Borre were evacuated during April, 1918, whilst a large portion of the St. Etienne shops were later handed over to the Nord Railway, whose northern shops were lost, to enable the French to cope with their repair work. The subsequent re-organisation carried out at St. Etienne, together with the loss of Borre, seriously affected the locomotive repair work and a large number of locomotives had to be sent to England for repairs.

New locomotive shops were hurriedly erected at Rang du Fliers, and by the end of September work was in operation at that place. As a precautionary measure, in case Audruicq had to be evacuated, a wagon repair depot was built at Cissel. This proved very useful in connection with the maintenance of British wagons, and was supplemented by a large number of outstation repair depots at various points to provide for the upkeep of W.D. stock.

The Beaurainville depot was sufficiently forward to permit of the storage of material by June 6th 1918, but the Lory depot was not completed, as the Allied counter-offensive in August rendered it unnecessary. Moreover, the Cissel depot, although primarily for the use of workshops at St. Etienne and Cissel, was utilised for the storage of standard gauge locomotive spare parts, and general stores for D.G.T. units in the neighbourhood of Rouen.

32. Improvised 'running sheds' could be constructed by experienced Light Railway Operating troops in as little as 24 hours, using readily available material such as corrugated iron. Dozens of such depots were constructed, then abandoned as the tide of war moved on. Wooden doors are a necessary precaution against Flanders weather! Visible in this view are two Hudson 0-6-0WT's, one Alco 2-6-2T, a Baldwin 4-6-0T and (right) a Hunslet 4-6-0T.
(Imperial War Museum, Q35519)

33. The resourceful Light Railway troops would also adapt existing buildings for railway purposes. This view shows what appears to be farm buildings, modified to form a quite palatial locomotive shed.
(Museum of Army Transport)

Stores

The rapid development of railway operations during 1917 resulted in a heavy increase in the work of the stores Department. In order to cope with the demands, extensive additional storage capacity had to be built. Accommodation at the Main Depot at Audruicq was doubled, and new depots were formed at Berguette for light railway material only, at Borre for standard gauge locomotive spare parts, and at Aire primarily for I.W.T. stores. In addition, new warehouses were erected at Audruicq, and arrangements made at Zeneghem for a depot for baulk timber, road sleepers and the overflow of standard gauge sleepers.

Small sectional stores were also provided in connection with the workshops at St. Etienne, and it was found necessary to have port storekeepers at Calais, Boulogne, Dieppe and Havre, and a Local Purchase Officer at Paris. Owing to the rapid increase of the storage requirements for the Transportation Services, the Stores Department was subsequently re-organised, all stores for all Directorates being placed under one central organisation, an A.D.G.T. (Stores) being located at G.H.Q., and administrating the whole of the Stores Department.

Personnel

The great development of railways and roads naturally demanded the provision of additional personnel. When the D.G.T. took over the responsibility for the transportation services at the end of 1916, there were only 52 sections in the Railway Directorate, this comprising 20 operating, 20 construction, and 12 R.T.E. sections, the total establishment being just over 13,000. In January, 1917, therefore, it became desirable to obtain heavy reinforcements and to divide the railway personnel into Railways and a Light Railways and Roads Directorates. Over 1,000 officers and 60,000 men were asked for, whilst the formation of additional Directorates necessitated an additional demand for nearly 100 units, totalling 20,000 officers and other ranks in April. The establishment was further supplemented by a later demand for 2,000 men to reinforce construction and operating companies.

Transportation Establishment in 1918

At the beginning of 1918, the effective strength of transportation troops in France was 2,290 officers and over 72,000 other ranks, this number subsequently being increased by heavy reinforcements following the enemy offensive in March. With the general retirement of the enemy during the autumn, the need for railway operating personnel was very acute, and the additional provision of skilled men from England became essential. In addition, arrangements were made to withdraw 3,000 men from the armies in France to form eight standard gauge railway operating companies and three standard gauge miscellaneous trade companies. By the time the first unit was formed, the need became less acute, owing to the fact that a certain amount of Belgian, French and German civilian labour had been obtained in the newly-occupied territory. As a result, only 1,300 men were withdrawn from the armies instead of 3,000 originally sanctioned.

The following statement shows the daily number of men working for the respective Transportation Services at various times during the year:-

34. A later view of the depot shows a line up of Baldwin 4-6-0T's, headed by No. 507, undergoing servicing.
(Museum of Army Transport)

Daily average number of men working

	May 1918	August 1918	November 1918	December 1918
Roads	25,045	28,592	40,745	34,449
Construction (S. and M. Gauge)	13,057	10,680	27,624	18,916
Docks	10,456	10,511	11,063	9,564
C.M.E.	671	902	2,713	2,816
I.W.T.	-	-	771	1,022
R.O.D.	1,323	1,162	1,915	1,797
Light Railways	2,265	5,909	1,541	1,663
Stores	1,552	1,660	2,193	2,084
C.E.P.C.	573	953	611	525
TOTAL	54,942	60,369	89,176	72,836

As will be noted, there was a very marked increase up to November, this being accounted for by the increased demands for road and standard gauge construction work. After the signing of the armistice, however, these demands naturally declined, with the result that the personnel working shows a marked diminution.

[1] *'Tractor' was the official British Army term for a petrol locomotive.*
[2] *A description of all steam and petrol locomotive types used by the WDLR, and a workslist of each class, may be found in "Narrow Gauge at War" (Plateway Press, 1987).*
[3] *This somewhat dubious reference presumably relates to the manufacture of petrol engines by W H Dorman Ltd, rather than of locomotives by Motor Rail, as the latter had only built railcars prior to 1916.*
[4] *'Or more' is believed to be an error, all engines employed being either two or four cylinder.*
[5] *Inland Waterways Transport.*

35. A line-up of 40hp Motor Rails, concentrated at a rear area location as light railway activity declined at the the end of 1918.
(Lens of Sutton)

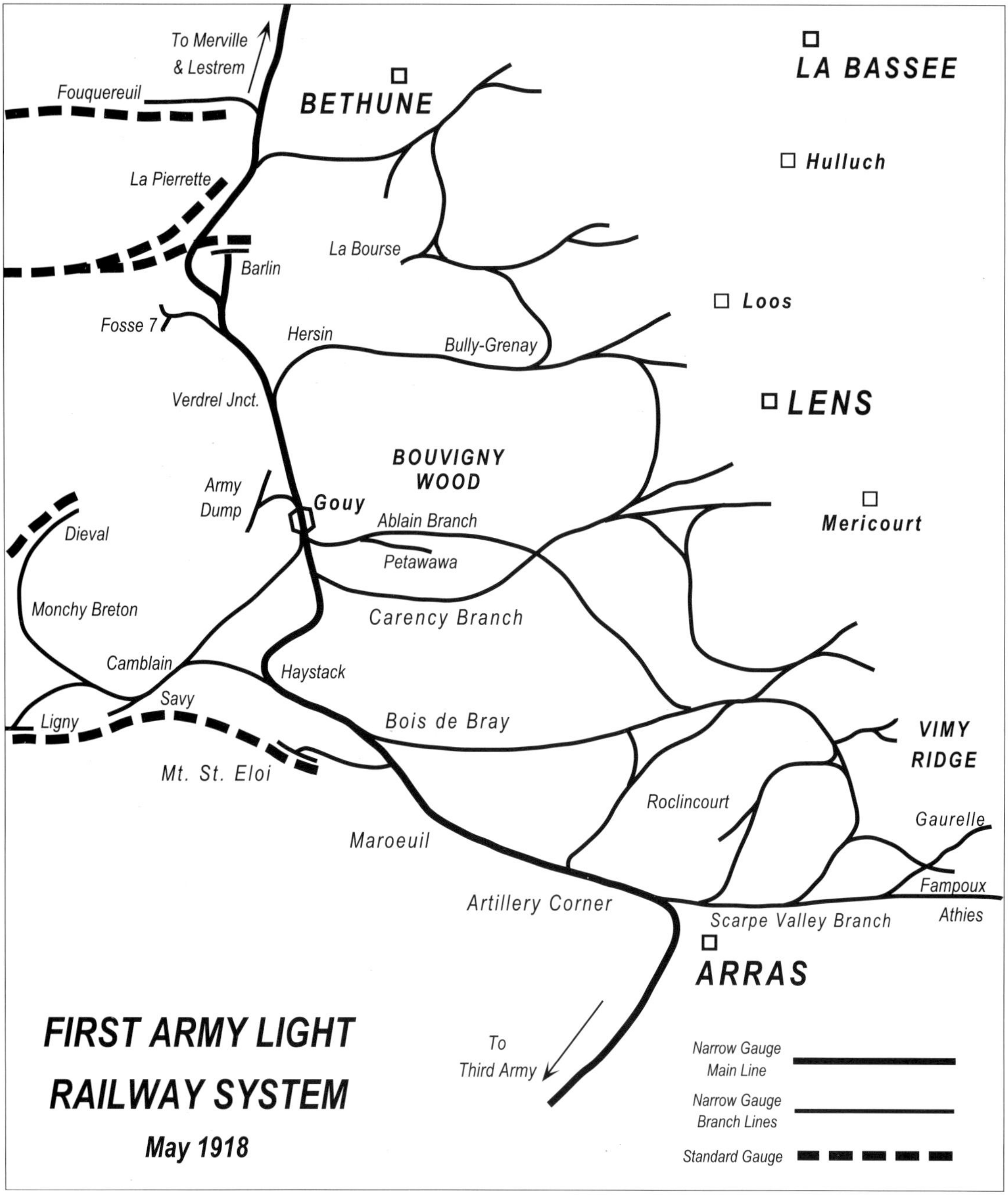

To Merville
& Lestrem
Fouquereuil
BETHUNE
LA BASSEE
Hulluch
La Pierrette
La Bourse
Barlin
Fosse 7
Hersin
Bully-Grenay
Loos
Verdrel Jnct.
LENS
BOUVIGNY
WOOD
Army
Dump
Gouy
Ablain Branch
Mericourt
Dieval
Petawawa
Monchy Breton
Carency Branch
Camblain
Haystack
Savy
Ligny
Bois de Bray
VIMY
RIDGE
Mt. St. Eloi
Roclincourt
Gaurelle
Maroeuil
Fampoux
Artillery Corner
Scarpe Valley Branch
Athies
ARRAS
FIRST ARMY LIGHT
RAILWAY SYSTEM
May 1918
To
Third Army
Narrow Gauge
Main Line
Narrow Gauge
Branch Lines
Standard Gauge

Chapter Two

"WHERE THE STRANGE ROADS GO DOWN"

Reminiscences of the British First Army Light Railways, 1917-18.

First published in the Railway Gazette Special War Transportation Number, dated 21 September 1920, reprinted by courtesy of Railway Gazette International.

THE FIRST ARMY LIGHT RAILWAY SYSTEM, shown in map 2, consisted of (1) a main line running roughly north to south from Bethune to Maroeuil, 4 miles west of Arras; (2) numerous branch lines running from various points on this main line eastwards towards our front-line infantry positions; and (3) an "escape" line running westwards from the southern end of the main line back to Savy, Ligny and Dieval, all on the standard gauge railway. The whole of the line was made up of single track, with the exception of a short stretch of main line at Gouy, where separate "up" and "down" roads had been laid, and, of course, at stations and passing places. The portion of main line at the southern end, from Bray Loop to Artillery Corner, was at one time worked by the Third Army, but was taken over from them by the First Army in April, 1917.

How the Operating Personnel Lived

The headquarters of the operating company with which I[1] was connected were situated at Maroeuil, near Arras, and when I arrived there the town was very badly damaged. The Chemin-der-fer du Nord standard gauge station was damaged very considerably, and the standard gauge railhead had, therefore, been moved back a couple of miles to Mont St. Eloi. A few days prior to my arrival a

36. Typical of the hundreds of transhipment points at which WDLR traffic was transferred from standard gauge to narrow gauge wagons. An 'open' 40hp Simplex positions a train of 'D' class wagons for loading.
(Museum of Army Transport)

37. A scene during the winter of 1917/18. Baldwin 4-6-0T No. 854 prepares to hand over its train to Armoured "Simplex" No. 2319, which is waiting in the background. (Lens of Sutton)

shell had twisted the substantial water column on the station platform like so much scrap iron. The personnel of the operating company at Maroeuil lived in wooden huts, sandbagged a portion of the way up as a protection against shrapnel and shell fragments. Dug-outs were available for shelter in the event of enemy shelling or air raids. The company's locomotive sheds and wagon shops were at Maroeuil, while the district traffic control office was located at Artillery Corner, near the village of Anzin, and midway between Maroeuil and Arras. At that time our front line positions were located roughly 4 miles east of Arras. It was at Artillery Corner that I made my home. All of us there lived in dug-outs constructed in the hillside, at the foot of which the River Scarpe placidly flowed eastwards, through Arras and towards the German lines. Behind us were the big guns, and in front the field guns.

Traffic Control

For the district traffic control office we had a roomy dug-out built in the hillside. Down the centre of the place ran a plain wooden table, at which sat the controllers and clerks. Along one wall was fixed the control board - a huge board painted black, with white grooves running along it to represent the railway system over which we worked, and with the name of each station, siding, dump, &c., painted in white letters in the proper place. Wire clips, to which a wooden tag was affixed, with the number of the engine painted thereon, were moved along the grooves on the board to coincide with the actual movements outside, as advised to district control over the telephone by the various outside control posts. Into these clips were placed specially printed slips of paper - one for each wagon - giving details as to wagon number, contents and station from and to. The information given on these slips was also transferred to the wagon books daily, and it was

38. Locomotive hauled trains could not safely operate right up to the guns they were serving, so shells were transhipped onto flat wagons, and hand pushed the last few hundred yards over trench tramways, to where they were needed.
(Museum of Army Transport)

thus possible to tell at a glance what traffic had been dealt with on any particular date.

The staff in the district control office worked in three shifts of eight hours each. On each shift were one sergeant in charge, two traffic controllers, two clerks and one telephone operator. The district went forward - that is, in an easterly direction - from Artillery Corner, through St. Nicholas just north of Arras, to Roclincourt, and so on to the foot of the Vimy Ridge, with a branch going off at St. Nicholas along the Scarpe Valley to Athies and Fampoux. Behind, it extended to Bois-de-Bray, from which point another operating company took over the traffic. Altogether there were about 20 miles of track, with extensive sidings at Artillery Corner and Maroeuil. Something like 16 outside control posts at different points on the line were staffed by us, and reported by telephone to the district control office at Artillery Corner the movements of all trains in their sections. Almost all of these control posts were located in dug-outs, varying in depth from 4 to 20ft. One of these dug-outs - that at Plateau, beyond Roclincourt and in sight of the enemy front line - in addition to serving as the light railway control post, also at times accommodated wounded walking cases from the trenches. During my stay in the district we inaugurated a system whereby the outside control staffs were given alternate spells of duty in the more advanced posts and those located further behind the front. The staff in the district control office were specially skilled, and remained on duty there throughout.

Traffic Working Incidents

In the rear areas behind Artillery Corner traffic was worked by steam locomotives, and on the forward lines beyond that point by 20 and 40hp petrol and petrol-electric tractors. About 1,000 tons of traffic was handled every 24 hours, consisting principally of ammunition, personnel, guns, rations, engineering material, poison gas cylinders, salvage and ballast for railway and road construction. Whatever happened, the batteries served by the light railway had, at all costs, to be fed. Their appetite, too, was phenomenal.

We had some rather exciting times running up shells for the guns at night. Looking backwards, it appears miraculous how sometimes the light railway trains managed to get through at all, for, often enough, enemy shells landed all around, on more than one occasion half burying the train

39. "As many as 35 men were conveyed in an ordinary narrow gauge open wagon..." These relaxed, and unarmed, troops appear to be travelling to (or from) 'rest and recreation'. Hunslet 4-6-0T No. 374 is at the head.
(Museum of Army Transport)

crew in flying debris. Our casualties were remarkably light: on one occasion a shell landed clean in the middle of a train of six wagons, smashing two of them to bits. The driver of the tractor hauling the train and the guard riding on the rear wagon, escaping unhurt, coolly set to and cleared the line, rerailed the tractor, which had come off the road, and carried on with the remaining four sound trucks.

Working in the dark on a derailment, not daring to show a light, and with enemy shells landing in the neighbourhood, and our own batteries firing right under our nose, was not exactly a picnic. It frequently happened that, after working on a derailed tractor or wagon for some time, it was found impossible to re-rail it before daylight, and so it had to wait until the following night, when a party would set off and finish the job, wondering the whole time whether the enemy would have noticed the tractor or wagon lying there during the day, and open up fire on the assumption that a party would go out at night to get the derailed vehicle on the line again

Description of Traffic

During my stay at Artillery Corner many thousands of troops were carried to and from the front. As many as 35 men were conveyed in an ordinary narrow gauge open wagon, and eight wagons usually formed a train load in this district. For the conveyance of artillery special steel gun bogies were utilised, and a train load of these would be made up of four, five or six loaded bogies, according to the size of the guns. The batteries invariably provided escorts to travel with each gun, and also labour to assist in loading and unloading. In times of stress the narrow gauge lines performed much useful work in conveying the guns back to a place of safety.

The ration traffic dealt with in the district travelled principally over the Scarpe Valley line towards Athies and Fampoux, skirting en-route the northern suburbs of Arras. This line was under direct

40. On 7th March 1918, the line has been cut by enemy shell fire. The driver of an 'open' 40hp Simplex feels his way gingerly along a still extant section of track. All being well, the breach will be repaired within 24 hours, and trains will be running again. (Museum of Army Transport)

observation from enemy balloons, and could only be worked at night. Four ration trains were loaded up daily at Maroeuil and Mont St. Eloi, and were hauled thence to Artillery Corner yard by steam locomotives. As soon as darkness fell, petrol locomotives conveyed the trains to their destination, which at one point was within rifle and machine gun range of the enemy line. On arrival there the wagons were unloaded by the infantry, and the empties hauled back to Artillery Corner or used for bringing troops back to rest billets.

The engineering material handled consisted principally of "elephant iron," wire netting, and cement for the construction of dug-outs and pill boxes, iron stakes, barbed wire and defence timber,

41. A Dick Kerr petrol electric has derailed on a substandard section of track, but luckily has plunged into soft mud, and appears little damaged. Sorting out a mishap like this became no more than a routine incident for the Light Railway Operating troops. (Museum of Army Transport)

42. The bonnet has been removed from this 20hp Simplex for routine maintenance, giving a useful view of the Dorman 2JO petrol engine, with magneto and water pump transversely mounted across the front. (Lens of Sutton)

and concrete slabs. All this was important traffic, but like everything else it had to give preference at times to ammunition.

The conveyance of loaded poison gas cylinders formed an interesting but rather dangerous part of the work performed by the light railways, and thousands of train loads of deadly gas were worked up to the liberating points by their aid. Much salved material, also, was brought down from the front by light railway to salvage dumps at standard gauge railheads, and considerable economies thereby effected.

A Traffic Exchange

At Artillery Corner traffic was exchanged with the Third Army, who held the adjoining portion of the front. The junction with that Army system was situated about half a mile east of Artillery Corner, the line branching off in a southerly direction, skirting the western portion of Arras and running

43. "The men...remained wonderfully cheerful." Despite the improvised conditions, and long hours of work, the Light Railway Operating troops were at least spared the worst privations of trench life, and most seemed to enjoy their jobs. Here, a maintenance crew poses with Alco 2-6-2T No. 1254. (Lens of Sutton)

44. A welcome break in the routine would be enjoyed when a captured enemy locomotive could be examined. This Deutz 10hp single cylinder petrol locomotive, one of a type used in large numbers by the German "feldbahns", has been cleaned up, ready to be shipped to central workshops for refurbishment, and possible use in WDLR service.
(Lens of Sutton)

45. Despite the primitive maintenance facilities, and the prevalent mud, efforts were usually made to keep the light railway locomotives clean. Baldwin 4-6-0T No. 747 receives a hose down at a running shed which (unusually) boasts an inspection pit. (Museum of Army Transport)

thence through Dainville to Simencourt. A most efficient telephone system enabled us to keep in touch with the Third Army controls in regard to traffic on and off that line.

Whilst on the subject of telephonic communication, mention should be made of the excellent work performed by the Signal Section of the Royal Engineers in this and other districts. To keep traffic moving, and so keep the guns going, and the front line positions supplied with men and material, it was at all times absolutely essential that telephonic communication from the district control office to the outside controls should be maintained. Time and again our telephone lines were severed by hostile shell fire, and no matter at what hour of the day or night this happened, the signal staff set out and made good the damage. How hazardous was their work may readily be realised.

The men at Artillery Corner, like so many other light railway units on detachment, away from company headquarters, were unfortunate by reason of the lack of facilities for amusement and recreation in the off hours at their disposal. Notwithstanding this, and the natural tendency to melancholia inseparable from dug-out life, they remained wonderfully cheerful. All were old railwaymen, and over occasional copies of the home railway publications they had many interesting discussions. Never once did they lose their interest in home railway affairs, and always were they eager for shop talk. Out in the control posts on the line there was usually a tattered copy of some railway publication or other lying about, and on the walls photographs galore of locomotives, stations and so on, clipped from magazines from time to time.

46. Out in the field, water supplies were a constant problem. Permanent water towers would provide an irresistible target for enemy artillery. Temporary facilities like this were quickly and easily constructed from sleepers and any standard issue army water tank. Water could also be taken, via the suction hose shown, from rivers, streams and shellholes. Three Baldwin 4-6-0T's queue for their turn at the tower.
(Museum of Army Transport)

47. The transport of wounded troops was an important function of the light railways. Many injured soldiers owed their lives to the speed with which the railways conveyed them to the nearest dressing station or field hospital. Facilities nearer the front line were inevitably primitive; here, the wounded men are loaded on to stretchers, balanced on the top of the ever-adaptable 'D' class wagon. In the background is a 120mm gun on a railway mounting.
(Imperial War Museum, Q6239)

Arming of the Railway Operating Troops

In view of the possibility of a sudden enemy break-through, the whole of the personnel of the First Army Light Railways were early in 1918 provided with rifles and bayonets, and opportunity taken to give them practice on the range. In connection with the possibility of a German break-through, our plans for the evacuation of the light railway locomotives and rolling-stock were all cut and dried, and every officer and senior non-commissioned officer was given an outline of the form this evacuation would take, and more definite instructions as to his own particular part in the operation. Had the Germans succeeded in breaking through the First Army positions in 1918, the chances are they would have secured little, if any, light railway rolling-stock; all stock would have been withdrawn behind our retiring troops, the lines blown up in vital places, and such works on the line as pumping stations, water tanks, locomotive sheds and the like rendered useless before the enemy arrived.

Gouy Marshalling Yards

At Gouy, some miles north of Artillery Corner, were situated the First Army Light Railway central marshalling yards. Here was the only stretch of double track on the whole of the main line in the Army area, and something like 800 loaded wagons per day were dealt with in the yards in addition to empties, traffic for all parts of the system passing through. The loaded wagons were sorted at Gouy and assembled in train loads for their various destinations. The yard was of the usual flat type; no gravitational yards existed, so far as I could learn, anywhere on the British light railways in France. It consisted of two portions - an up and a down yard - the former dealing principally with traffic going toward the front, and the latter with the return traffic. In the up yard there were five roads, each capable of accommodating about 30 wagons; and in the down yard four slightly shorter lines. Empties were collected into train loads in the down yard, and any slight damages made good on the spot by the wagon repair staff, serious damages being left to the wagon shop staff at Barlin, 6 miles to the north, where the headquarters of the First Army Light Railways were situated. Shunting operations were performed by the ordinary train engines.

All kinds of traffic passed through Gouy, and as it was no infrequent occurrence for a stray enemy aeroplane to come over in the daytime, the yards were invariably kept as free from traffic as possible. Often at busy times, however, there would be as many as 80 or 100 wagons of high-explosive shells standing in the up sidings at the same time waiting engine-power to lift them. A very large troop movement in the district or the working of trains of gas cylinders up to the front in preparation for a big attack, which drew the locomotives away from their ordinary work, usually resulted in congestion at Gouy. We were most fortunate, however, as regards our freedom from enemy shell fire. If a shell from the enemy had dropped on our yard at times of pressure, there would have been very little left of Gouy. Only once, however, did a shell land anywhere in the immediate vicinity, and this demolished a well which had been sunk in the down yard to obtain water for the locomotives, smashing up in addition the pump-house alongside. It always struck me as an inexplicable thing why the enemy did not shell the Gouy yards in earnest, for he must have known quite well of their existence. In addition to the observation aeroplanes which came over, it was possible on a clear day to see his balloons, and from them he could not have failed to watch the movements of trains in and out.

Camouflage

In connection with enemy observation from the air, and consequent shelling, an interesting occurrence arose at Bois-de-Bray, a little to the south of Gouy. The enemy frequently used to shell a duckboard track there leading to an old, disused infantry camp, and we often wondered at his

48. A greater degree of comfort is provided by a standard bogie wagon, modified to carry three stretcher cases, with space for attendants, or any 'walking wounded', in the other half of the car. Hunslet 4-6-0T No. 318 is the motive power. (Museum of Army Transport)

partiality for this target, for the light railway a short distance away was rarely hit. Eventually a photograph came into our possession taken by an enemy airman, and on the explanatory notes alongside being examined, it was discovered that the duckboard track in question had been mistaken by the German intelligence staff for an important light railway. No reference was made on the map to the light railway proper.

The ballast for the First Army light railways was obtained from a colliery near Barlin called Fosse 7, the slag heaps being reached by a line of light railway about half a mile in length, leaving the main line between Verdrel and Cairo Junction. The slag, which was loaded into light railway trucks both by hand and by means of a steam navvy manufactured by Ruston Hornsby, Limited, Lincoln, made excellent light railway ballast, and loadings often touched 1,000 tons per day.

Light Railway Reorganisation

On the Fifth Army being reorganised after the retirement on the Amiens front in the spring of 1918, it took over the portion of front lying between Bethune and Armentieres, and the light railway system was quickly developed in this area. The northern section, with which the writer was connected, made its headquarters at La Lacque, about 2 miles north west of Berguette. As shown in map 3, the light railway system then consisted of a main north to south line running from La Lacque to Bethune, with a connection at its southern end with the First Army system, and branch lines running eastwards from this lateral towards the infantry position. At the outset the northern section simply served an engineering dump on the standard gauge at La Lacque and an ammunition dump further west at Neufpré, which had also standard gauge connection, and which was situated on the outskirts of the town of Aire-sur-le-Lys. The last portion of track between Neufpré and Aire was only

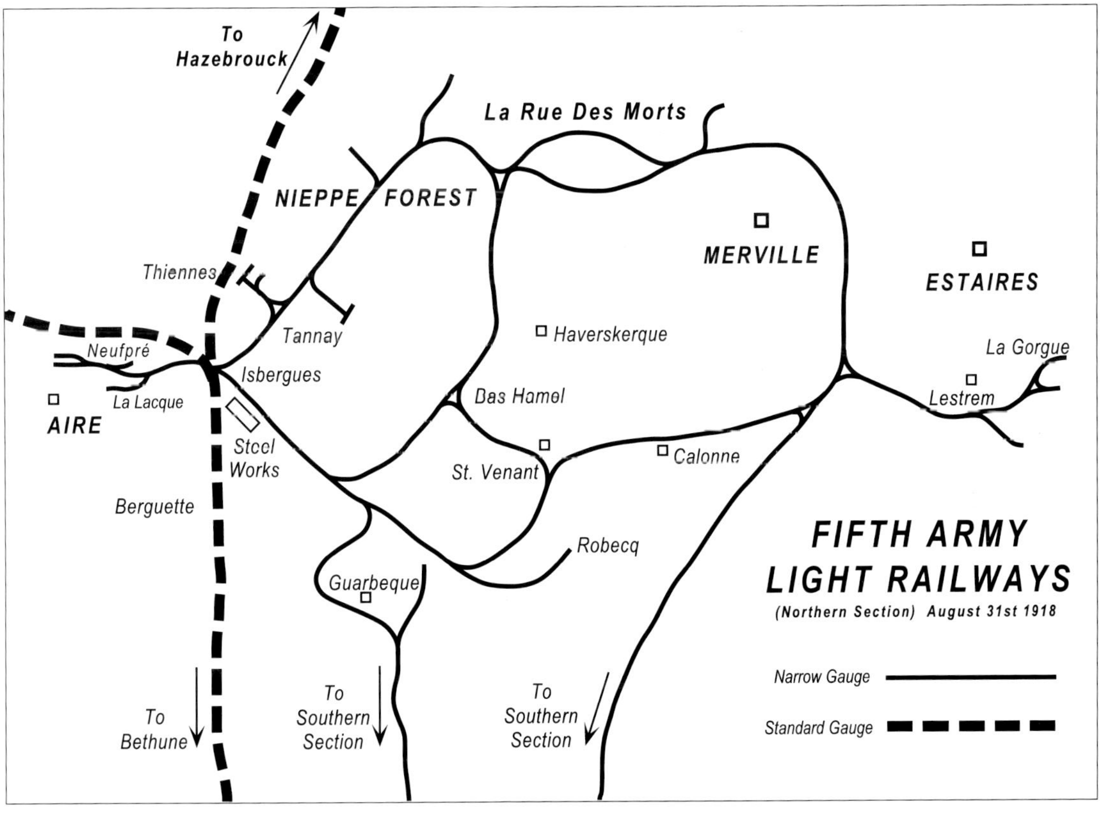

49. During the German offensive in the spring of 1918, large sections of the Allied 60cm gauge networks were overrun, and equipment captured or damaged. This view, taken near Pozieres, shows an almost unscathed Hunslet 4-6-0T, plus two Baldwins, the nearer of which has been blown off the track by a 'near miss' from an artillery shell. (Eisenbahnarchiv)

suitable for the passage of trucks pushed by hand, and was used for the transport of material to a bridging school of the Royal Engineers on the Lys Canal, and an R.E. electric power-station. The engineering dump at La Lacque was formed on what had been the site of the central light railway workshops. These shops were enormous places, full of costly machinery of every description for the repair of steam and petrol locomotives, and rolling-stock, and when first laid down our front line infantry positions were 20 miles distant. When the enemy made his advance there in the spring of 1918 the place was evacuated, and the shops transferred to a safer site at Beaurainville, between Hesdin and Etaples. The enemy shelled the La Lacque workshops at the time of his advance, but practically the whole of the shops and their contents were safely transferred to Beaurainville.

About a couple of miles to the south-east of La Lacque were situated the Isbergues steel works, run by the French, the second largest works of its kind in the country. These works continued to employ many hands, and turned out large quantities of steel - approximately one-sixth of their pre-war output - despite daily enemy shelling and bombing. Soon after our arrival at La Lacque we commenced to open up a light railway line running from that point, and passing through Isbergues, to the south-western corner of the Nieppe Forest and through the forest towards Merville. The forest was entered about 2 miles north-east of Isbergues steel works, near the village of Tannay. Just prior to entering the forest a branch left the main line and went to Thiennes, on the Hazebrouck-Isbergues standard gauge line. At Thiennes there was at first simply an R.A.M.C.[2] casualty clearing station and an engineering dump, but as time went on the place was opened out as a standard gauge railhead, and troops and ration traffic were dealt with in considerable quantities.

Although the line from La Lacque to the Nieppe Forest had been in existence some time, little had been done prior to our arrival to develop traffic over it. The ammunition dump at Neufpré and the La Lacque engineering dump were, however, soon opened up seriously; numerous light railway locomotives were put into traffic and a stock of wagons got together, and in a couple of weeks or thereabouts we were carrying well over a thousand tons of traffic daily. There was only one main road through the Nieppe forest, and alongside this was laid the light railway track. On either side was dense forest with thick, tangled vegetation under the trees, with here and there narrow, winding footpaths leading into the heart of the forest. Along many of these paths the light railway track was laid for the purpose of conveying shells to the batteries concealed in the forest. After passing the "Street of the Dead," the light railway line continued to within about a mile of the eastern edge of the forest opposite Merville.

Light Railway Extension on Enemy Retirement

About the middle of August the enemy commenced to retire on this front, and by the beginning of September we had pushed ahead with the narrow gauge line as far as the northern outskirts of Merville, the enemy being then back at Estaires. Until this retirement took place the main road through the forest, along which ran the light railway line, was under direct observation from the enemy balloons, and to conceal to some extent our movements strips of canvas about 6ft wide were stretched from tree to tree across the road at a height of about 10ft from the ground. As the enemy retired, we quickly pushed the light railway forward, and by the beginning of September opened up a line which branched off in a south-easterly direction at Isbergues, and after following the Aire Canal for some 3 miles, proceeded to St. Venant, Calonne, Lestrem, the southern outskirts of Merville, and on to La Gorgue. Huge quantities of light railway and road material were rushed up the light railway to keep pace with the retreating enemy, and new traffic controls were constantly established further east as the line grew. After passing Calonne the new line was laid on our old light railway formation, and alongside the new track were the old rails, broken, twisted and torn up by the enemy to hamper our pursuit. On our old lines we came across numerous British wagons which had been captured by the enemy in the spring, many of them quite intact, and these were quickly put into traffic.

The construction of the light railway lines in this district presented a good many engineering difficulties, for although there were practically no gradients, canals, streams and marshy ground abounded. During September, 1918, heavy rains seriously interfered with the work of construction and played havoc with newly ballasted track.

50. When the Allied breakthrough came at last, large sections of light railway ceased to have any useful function, and track and sleepers were recovered for use elsewhere. This working party, which includes some black (probably West Indian) troops, is using a train powered front and rear by 'protected' Simplexes, to recover track panels. (Lens of Sutton)

Fifth Army Light Railways Left Behind

The retreat of the enemy, begun in August, continued throughout September, 1918, and by the end of that month the Fifth Army light railways were left high and dry miles behind the front, in spite of the efforts of the construction troops to lay steel. As, however, the main ammunition and engineering material dumps, and infantry rest-camps, were also situated at an equally great distance from the fighting line, the light railways continued to carry considerable quantities of traffic, including large numbers of troops, up to the end of steel, from which point road transport was employed. New dumps were gradually made further forward, but as our fighting forces were almost daily moving eastward on the heels of the retreating enemy, no permanent dumps could be made, as an advanced dump with light railway connection laid out one day would be miles behind the front the next. The light railway line by the end of September was being operated as far as Laventie and Fromelles, almost within sight of Lille.

With a haul from standard gauge railhead at La Lacque to end of steel of nearly 20 miles, over a considerable proportion of newly laid track, it was somewhat difficult to meet all traffic requirements, particularly as the power and wagon-stock remained the same as had been employed on a small self-contained system with an extreme haul of 8 or 10 miles. At this period train crews worked exceptionally long hours, and if two trips per day per train from standard gauge railhead to end of steel were obtained it was considered good work, especially as labour for loading and unloading trucks was particularly scarce. We had been an exceptionally long way behind the infantry since the beginning of September, but with the capture of Lille on October 18, 1918, our light railways were hopelessly out of the fight. The lay-out at the end of October is shown in map 4. Headquarters were then moved up to Lestrem, and steam working introduced as far as Fournes, 6 miles south-west of Lille, while trains drawn by petrol locomotives travelled to Lomme on the town's north-western outskirts.

German Light Railways

The light railway line from Lestrem to Lomme consisted mainly of German track. As the enemy retired he did not damage the track to any extent. Here and there sections of rail had been removed,

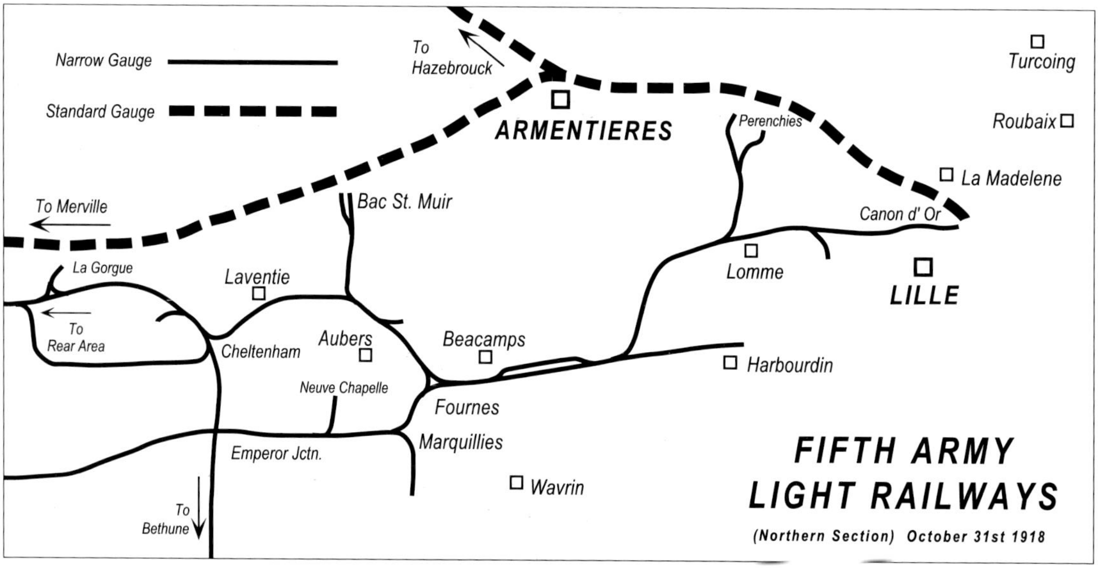

but these were quickly restored, and thus he left at our disposal a most useful light railway system, which we at once commenced to use for the transport of ammunition and material.

After leaving Lestrem the line passed through the ruins of the town of Laventie, and then turned in a south-easterly direction over the Aubers Ridge to Fournes, on the La Basse-Lille road. Here it turned off to the north-east to Harbourdine and Lomme, to the west of Lille. Between Fournes and Harbourdine the enemy left an excellent double track some 3 or 4 miles in length, equipped with semaphore signals worked from substantially-built brick signal-boxes alongside. Every signal-box and station had its name-board outside in German, and all along the line were speed indicators, warning boards and the like. Everywhere were spurs leading to various camps and artillery positions, indeed, the whole district was one vast network of light railway completed and in course of construction.

At Lomme was an extensive light railway yard with large, brick built locomotive and wagon shops lit by electricity, and full of tools and spare parts. Huge stocks of coal had been left behind, a hundred light railway wagons, and immense quantities of rails, sleepers and ballast. From Lomme the line branched off in two directions. The line to the north went to Perenchies and the other branch to Canon D'or, just outside the citadel of Lille. Here the line was blocked by the standard

51. Light railways followed the 'lie of the land' as far as possible, being little troubled by minor obstacles such as buildings. Some could be demolished, but here the narrow gauge rails thread through a convenient archway in the ruined building. The scene is near Arras on 8th March 1918. (Museum of Army Transport)

gauge railway, which had been blown up by the enemy. These lines were all being operated when news was received of the signing of the armistice, and on November 13 ammunition traffic began to be worked back from Lille to Lestrem. All along the light railway system the same backward movement was soon in progress.

General Utility of Narrow Gauge Lines

Narrow gauge lines were not confined exclusively to the forward area, for there was an extensive light railway system on the lines of communication in France. At Oissel, near Rouen, timber was worked by 60cm railway from the Rouvray Forest to standard gauge. At Brotonne, midway between Rouen and Le Havre, a short narrow gauge line served to convey timber from forest to Inland Water Transport barges on the River Seine[3]. At Havre light railways dealt with petrol and general stores, and a small system at Trouville-sur-Mer served convalescent depots and hospitals.

From the date of their inception light railways were concerned in every success of our arms, and played no small part in civilisation's struggle. I should like, in conclusion, to take this opportunity of paying a tribute to the loyalty of the whole of the light railway staff - most of them drawn from the home railways - with whom I came in contact in France. Always cheerful, always anxious to put their last ounce of energy into whatever task they might be allotted, it was indeed a pleasure to command a body of such men. Casualties were inevitable, but the memory of those very gallant railwaymen who paid the supreme sacrifice will ever be with us.

[1] *These reminiscences are uncredited but are believed to be the work of Arthur L Stead, who wrote a similar (but much abbreviated) account in "The Locomotive" magazine in 1946.*

[2] *Royal Army Medical Corps.*

[3] *There were considerably more timber railways than are mentioned here, many of them operated by the Canadian Forestry Corps. More details are given in a later Chapter in this book and also in "The Kerry Tramway and other Timber Light Railways" (Plateway Press, 1992).*

52. Australian gunners are enduring the double heat of a French summer's day, and the working of a big gun. The prompt support given to the Allied effort by ANZAC and other Dominion forces was a source of great pride, and these troops are regularly featured on 'propaganda' postcards published during the war.
(Author's collection)

Chapter Three

ANZAC ENTERPRISE ON THE TWO FOOT GAUGE

The Australian Light Railway Operating Companies, 1917-18.

AUSTRALIA AND NEW ZEALAND'S DECLARATIONS OF WAR were almost simultaneous with that of Great Britain, and both countries set about raising expeditionary forces. Only volunteers were accepted, and the bulk of the initial Australian Imperial Force (AIF) were existing militiamen (territorials). The New Zealand Force was recruited mainly from their militia, and in some cases whole regimental units volunteered to a man. Australia ultimately sent 416,000 troops - out of a population of less than seven million, a higher proportion of the population than any other country but Britain herself. 59,342 men of the AIF paid the ultimate price and a further 152,000 were injured - a total casualty rate exceeding 50%! Of the New Zealand Expeditionary Force,16,654 were killed and 41,317 wounded.

The ANZACs (Australian and New Zealand Army Corps) were first in action at Gallipoli, Turkey, in April 1915, and were later deployed in France, Belgium and in the Middle East. Major battles in which they took part include Pozières, the Somme, Bullecourt, Messines and Third Ypres (Passchendaele).

Railwaymen rush to join up

Australian railwaymen were as eager as any to enlist in the colours, but the high physical and medical standards demanded of recruits for the AIF meant that many older railwaymen were unable to join up in 1914 and 1915. This changed in 1916 when the British War Office decided to expand the military railways in France, but, finding that insufficient trained railwaymen were available, asked the Dominions to help.[1]

Faced with recruiting difficulties following heavy casualties at Gallipoli and in France, Australia initially declined to assist, but the War Office asked for this to be reconsidered, as specialist troops

53. Although of indifferent technical quality, this photo is of interest in being one of the few to depict New Zealand troops at work on a light railway. Running repairs are being carried out on Alco 2-6-2T No. 1251. (Collection – R T Horne)

for railway duties would not have to meet the rigorous physical standards required for combat troops. The Australian Government then agreed, and volunteers to raise a railway unit for service on the Western Front were called for in November 1916. The response was overwhelming; without waiting to be asked, volunteers had been submitting their names since October, and every major State railway system offered to sponsor a railway unit for overseas service. Both operating and engineering staff were required, and one incentive was rapid promotion from cleaner to fireman, or from fireman to driver; also about half those recruited would be appointed non-commissioned officers. The huge volunteer response led Australia to offer four railway units instead of one.

Recruiting and basic military training were conducted in December 1916 and early 1917. The four units, plus a fifth raised in early 1917, embarked for service overseas between January and May 1917. In view of the necessity to work closely with British WDLR units while in France, it was deemed necessary for the newly-raised Australian units to undergo further 'railway' training at Longmoor, which took place in the spring of 1917; thus it was mid 1917 before the first troops were deployed on active service in France.

Meanwhile, however, on the Western Front, the need for railway operating troops was so desperate that the AIF raised the 1st ANZAC Light Railway Operating Company from volunteers among the Australian and New Zealand troops already serving in France (these would have included a sprinkling of experienced railwaymen young and fit enough to have satisfied the recruiting criteria in 1914 and 1915). This unit went into service officially in March 1917. Also, as will be seen in Chapter 8, ANZAC personnel had been building and operating light railways, on the Suez front, from as early as 1916. A full list of the Australian railway companies involved in operating light railways - showing their frequent changes of name - is contained in Table 1.

Although the Australian railwaymen's experience and training was exclusively in 'main line' railway operations, it was necessary, following the massive expansion of Light Railway organisation (described in Chapter 1), to designate several of the Australian units as Light Railway Operating Companies. Basic training in light railway operating procedures would have been carried out at Longmoor, and the other skills required simply 'learned' in the field. A typical LROC would have a complement of 3-5 officers and 260-270 men, and the official war establishment of an Australian LROC is summarised, by trade, in Table 2. This has some detail variations by comparison with the

Table 1: Names of Australian Light Railway Units

Date	Title
January 1917	2nd Section, Australian Railway Troops
August 1917	15th Australian Lt Rly Operating Company
March 1918	1st Australian Lt Rly Operating Company
March 1917	5th Section, Australian Railway Troops
August 1917	16th Australian Lt Rly Operating Company
March 1918	2nd Australian Lt Rly Operating Company
March 1917	1st ANZAC Lt Rly Operating Company
June 1917	17th ANZAC Lt Rly Operating Company
January 1918	17th Australian Lt Rly Operating Company
March 1918	3rd Australian Lt Rly Operating Company
September 1918	3rd Australian Lt Rly (Forward) Company

initial organisation copied from the Royal Engineers; blockmen, number takers, porters, steam raisers, a timekeeper, a caller up, a painter and a tailor, were among those not deemed necessary by the Australians, while rail traffic clerks,a pay clerk and a postal clerk are among those added. Another curiosity is the distinctly un-railway like position of Regimental Sergeant Major, not deemed necessary in a British LROC. It seems probable that the Australians recognised the need for military guidance in a unit recruited entirely from civilian tradesmen, without the leavening of traditional military experience that would be found in a British unit raised from the Royal Engineers.

The first Australian railway units into action often had to improvise with left-over equipment, and, lacking any text books or reliable instructions, had to establish the efficacy (or otherwise) of the equipment provided by 'trial and error,' in which many valuable lessons were learned, to be passed on to the units later deployed in France. An early report[2] on the XVII Corps light railway system records:

"The line was taken over from the French in March 1916, 47 kilometres, the southern sector having just been completed. The rolling-stock taken over from the French was as follows:

2 locomotives in general disrepair
1 French tractor and 2 trailers (the trailer with the broken axle)
48 double bogie wagons with narrow superstructure
6 tip wagons

A quantity of heavy bogies, not in running order, were afterwards found at various points on the line, also bogies and bodies of tip wagons needing large repairs.

The present rolling stock is as follows:

3 locos in good running order, English "Hudsons"
4 French petrol tractors carrying 2 tons and hauling total of 4 tons up 1 in 7

Table 2: Breakdown of Tradesmen - Australian LROC

Blacksmiths and strikers	6	Foremen	1
Boilermakers and assistants	6	Guards and brakesmen	42
Boilerwashers and packers	3	Orderlies	5
Bootmakers	1	Outdoor inspector	1
Breakdown gang	1	Payclerk	1
Chargemen	3	Postal clerk	1
Clerks	5	Pumpers, coalmen, labourers	16
Controllers and Station Masters	11	Quartermaster sergeant	1
Cooks	6	Rail traffic clerks	12
Coppersmiths and Tinsmiths	1	Regimental Sergeant Major	1
Draftsmen (locomotive)	1	Sanitation	3
Drivers (internal combustion)	24	Shunters	20
Drivers (steam)	27	Storemen	4
Electric fitters	2	Wagon examiners	9
Firemen	26	Wagon repairers	7
Fitters and assistants, turners	18	TOTAL	265

(1 under repair,1 more is expected)
4 trailers each carrying 2 tons
1 British 20hp Simplex tractor, used for shunting and track inspection
(will haul 4 tons up 1 in 80)
53 double bogie wagons
8 double bogie wagons with wide platforms
8 double bogie box cars
6 single bogie box cars
18 tip wagons

The locomotives are used on the Maroeil-Mont St. Eloy-Bois de Bray section as they can run by day. The tractors run as far as 'Birmingham' and on occasions 'Cabaret Rouge'. It depends on circumstances whether it is advisable to take them this far or not, as they are somewhat noisy in low gear. It appears however that the enemy sometimes mistakes them for aircraft engines.

The 20hp British tractor has not yet been tried on the light track, but will probably not be too heavy if the track is well ballasted. At first the adhesion of this tractor was very deficient, but this was afterwards improved at Audricq by the addition of weights. The double bogie Decauville wagons keep the rails well, have heavy dead weight for the weight carried and they require heavy track at 16lb/yard. The use of 9lb track precludes the operation of steam locos.This has been proved by experiences of ROD at Savy, and it is doubtful if it (ie 9lb track) will take the tractors.

54. 16th (later 2nd) Australian LROC transferring ammunition from standard gauge to light railway at Frizeville, near Poperinghe, Belgium, October 1917. Baldwin 4-6-0T No. 667 is one of three batches delivered between February and April 1917 and originally numbered in the series 1005-1150. (Australian War Memorial, C1357)

55. A scene packed full of detail and interest, for the modeller in particular! It depicts the marshalling yard of the 15th (later 1st) Australian LROC near Ypres in June 1917. The locomotives – 16 are visible – are mainly Baldwins and Alcos, the one on the left boasts some crude weather protection. Note the well laid sleepered track, and the method of watering the loco from a standpipe. (Australian War Memorial, C1388)

A great difficulty is that often a portion of line (re-alignment, deviation etc.) has to be laid under difficulties and in the dark, and it is sometimes necessary to use it before it can properly be ballasted. Light track is then apt to become distorted and even unusable. The steepest grade is 1 in 7, which is excessive for good working. 1 in 10 may be taken as a ruling grade, 1 in 15 if possible."

Light Railways on the offensive

The relaxed physical standards for recruiting the railwaymen may have engendered a belief that they were in for an 'easy' war. In practice, however, the Australian railwaymen - like their colleagues in British, Canadian and (later) American units, found that they were very much in the front line. Casualties were caused by shellfire, aircraft attack, and by the hazards of railway operating work itself. By way of example, casualties for the 17th ANZAC Light Railway Operating Company for the month of October 1917 were 9 killed and 26 wounded - out of a strength of less than 300 men. But, as the following extracts from War Diaries and official reports reveal, there were opportunities to hit back at the enemy; and there were lighter moments to enliven an otherwise dull routine…

"To: Officer Commanding 2 Australian Light Railway Company

As I understand that several units are claiming that their AA guns brought down the enemy plane in your vicinity last night, I am writing to say that I and another officer were outside when the plane was over, and from the direction it came and after making a turn (the tracer bullets from your gun were plainly visible) your gun was the only one that located it. We distinctly saw the bullets from your gun on the plane, then it burst into flames. I wanted to let you know that your gunner should have the satisfaction of knowing he had as much or more claim to the destruction of the plane as anyone else.

(Sgd) W Sears, Major
Area Commandant, Crombeke" [3]

Gas warfare - on the 60cm gauge

"On the night of June 22nd/23rd (1918) seven trains consisting of 49 specially prepared 'B' class trucks, each containing 40 cylinders, and hauled by 40hp tractors, left Pedelhoek 7.30 p.m. for Trois Bois, where trucks were man handled by infantry parties to two points a further distance of 200 yards or 500 yards ahead of the front line - the tractors which had been detached, meanwhile standing in the sidings at Tros Bois. Each cylinder had a detonator attached, and were joined up with insulated copper wire, and electrically discharged from the trucks by means of a battery. The discharge took place a little after midnight. The gas should escape normally in 15 minutes, but an

56. Track control board of the 16th (later 2nd) Australian LROC at Westhoek, near Ypres, October 1917.
(Australian War Memorial, C1393)

57. Alco 2-6-2T No. 1217 draws gingerly through the ruins of a devastated village near Ypres with a ballast train for the 17th (later 3rd) Australian LROC, in October 1917. (Australian War Memorial, C1362)

hour elapsed before the trucks could be withdrawn, and then all personnel engaged had to resort to the box respirator – train crews had to wear them throughout the whole homeward journey. The whole of the trucks were safely withdrawn without being molested, a sure sign that the enemy had been severely dealt with.

(A further) attack was made on the night of July 23rd/24th, with 2,500 cylinders, conveyed in 63 'B'class wagons, hauled by 9 tractors. The trains were exposed to a lot of enfilading enemy machine gun fire from the right flank on reaching Austral Siding, and several men who were riding on the trucks were wounded – the solid steel armour alone saved the tractor drivers, as many bullets struck the machines.[4] The last train of empty cylinders did not get away until 3.20am, owing to a derailment in 'No Mans Land,' and we were subjected to heavy shelling, probably retaliation.

(A further) attack was made on the night of 26th/27th August with 2,500 cylinders in the same place as the first one, and was attended with the usual good result and fortune as far as Light Railway personnel were concerned, but the Americans, who were occupying this part of the front, and who supplied the pushing parties, sustained numerous casualties, principally from the effects of our own gas, through their not taking the proper precautions. One man was found dead alongside the last train when it was drawn out, and several succumbed subsequently. The leading tractor of the convoy on this occasion had a flat wheel, and an upward exhaust, and the noise evidently attracted the attention of the "Hun", as red, green and white rockets immediately ascended from his line, followed by a heavy bombardment. The noisy tractor was detached, and side tracked in Castle Siding. The following trains were promptly taken out of the shelled area to avoid possible mishap. On the return home the last train of seven trucks of loaded cylinders met with a mishap, through the above mentioned tractor refusing to negotiate the curve, as a result it overbalanced, dragging two trucks with it; these were quickly rerailed by a brake down gang which accompanied the trains on each occasion."[5]

An embarrassing interlude

"June 29th. At 2 p.m. today the Unit was inspected by General Sir W A Birdwood KCB. There were 150 men on parade. The General expressed his extreme pleasure with the general appearance and bearing of the unit and congratulated the unit on their fine work during the first strenuous months. Whilst the GOC was addressing the troops a serious accident occurred on the spot. A train of personnel was proceeding from Vox Vrie direction towards Heidebecke and when about 80 yards from the parade a truck door dropped and catching on a sleeper, turned over and derailed the other three trucks.

58. Evidence of the destruction wrought by enemy artillery: the marshalling yard of the 16th (later 2nd) Australian LROC at Birr Crossroads, near Ypres, after shelling, 16th-20th October 1917. A damaged 40hp Simplex and train is at right. The yard was then abandoned and traffic transferred to the yard at 'Hellfire Corner', deemed, apparently, in spite of its name, safer. (Australian War Memorial, C1356)

59. The scant protection provided by the 'open' Simplex is apparent from this view of MR 2145, a casualty of the artillery attack at Birr Crossroads described in the previous illustration. (Australian War Memorial, C1400)

Fortunately no serious injuries resulted. No. 1 maintenance gang replaced sleepers, 3 lengths of rail and had the line completely reopened by 4pm. General Birdwood expressed his surprise at the rapidness of the work done, and his favourable appreciation of the way in which the crew responded to the call."[6]

[1] *Much of this account is adapted from "Australian Railwaymen at War" by John Bullen, published in the ARHS "Bulletin", September and October 1995.*

[2] *Condensed from "Report on XVII Corps 60cm Light Railway System," by Captain K D Galbraith, for Brigadier General DA&QMG Corps, 8th April 1916. Courtesy Australian War Memorial, Canberra.*

[3] *Extract from Routine Order No. 270, 28th July 1918, Captain G A Gahan, Officer Commanding 2nd LROC. Courtesy Australian War Memorial.*

[4] *The locomotives were presumably Armoured Simplexes. This is the only account known to the author describing these locomotives in action, and seems to demonstrate the effectiveness of the protection – against rifle fire, at least.*

[5] *Condensed from a report by A/OC 2nd Australian LROC's, dated 9th February 1919, listing all gas attacks in which the Company was involved. Courtesy Australian War Memorial.*

[6] *Extract from War Diary, 2nd Australian LROC, June 1918. Courtesy Australian War Memorial.*

60. On April 11th 1917 the Fifth Army launched an assault against the Hindenberg line, south of Arras, in Belgium. The 4th Australian Division was included in the attack against Bullecourt, and succeeded in breaching the enemy's defences. This view, taken on 19th April 1917 on the Bapaume road, shows the effectiveness of the light railways In moving large quantities of men forward. (IWM, E (Aus) 468)

61. Baldwin 4-6-0T No. 652, one of the penultimate batch ordered for the WDLR, hauls a five wagon load near Cardonette on 28th July 1918. (IWM, E (Aus) 2768)

Chapter Four

TRAMWAY TRACKS AND FOREST RAILS

The Canadian Tramway and Forestry Corps.

CANADA'S FIRST EXPEDITIONARY FORCE of 33,000 men - effectively a call-up of the existing militia units - was mustered, armed and sent to Europe within two months of the outbreak of war. Pivotal battles in which the Canadians took part include those at Ypres, Festubal, Givency, Courcelette and of course the Somme. Their proudest moment probably came when Byng's Canadian Corps finally took Vimy Ridge on April 9th 1917, as part of the Arras offensive that ultimately led to Allied ascendancy over the German forces.

Tramway pioneers

The Canadians were great- one might say compulsive - railway builders. Eventually some 12,000 men, including three battalions of Railway Construction Corps, a Railway Bridging Company and 13

62. Reading of the horrors of the Passchendaele campaign still has the power to shock, even 80 years after the event. Driving rain and bitter cold made conditions even more hellish than the norm, and constant toil was needed to keep the light railways serviceable in these conditions. A Dick Kerr petrol electric prepares to move off with a train carrying two naval guns on narrow gauge transporters. (Canadian 'official,' CO3751)

63. A more cheerful scene is presented in April 1917 as the first train runs over Vimy Ridge following its capture during the Arras offensive. Two near new 20hp Simplexes provide the motive power: the first carries an (unofficial?) painted number '98' which cannot be reconciled with any lists. The enthusiastic driver has also 'scrounged' a motor car horn to announce his passage. (Canadian 'official,' CO1259)

64. Railway construction (I): Canadian troops recover spoil from buildings wrecked by shellfire, and load it onto a train, headed by a 20hp Simplex, for use in extending or consolidating the narrow gauge line. 'Proper' railway ballast was only sporadically available, so improvised substitutes like this were often used. (Canadian 'official,' CO2088)

Railway construction (II): A new length of trackbed is being 'graded' using a team of horses. An American pattern side tipping wagon (WDLR class 'L') stands ready to supply ballast when needed. On the right is a train of 18-pounder field guns on their special wagons. (Canadian 'official,' CO3807)

66. A panoramic view of the Canadian Tramways Corps yard at Villers-au-Bois, in the First Army Area. The marshalling yard contains a good selection of the types of wagon used by the WDLR, and loads identifiable include boxed rifle ammunition and pit props. This is one of the relatively few views available showing a steam locomotive in use with the Canadian forces. (Canadian 'official,' CO3809)

67. Using petrol locomotives reduced the problem of water supply for the locos. But water still had to be carried for the troops, and this view shows an 'H' class tank wagon, holding 1,500 Imperial gallons, being filled at a primitive water supply point. (Canadian 'official,' CO2423)

battalions of railway operating troops were employed in France. The bulk of these were employed on standard gauge railways, where the experience of those troops with a railroad background would be of more direct relevance. However one LROC (the 13th) was composed entirely of Canadian personnel, and this was deployed in France from 9th June 1917.

From a much earlier date, however, Canadian troops began making maximum use of trench tramways which they inherited from French units that they relieved, and extending these to cover other sections of their front lines. Anticipating the setting up of Light Railway Operating Companies, the Canadian 2nd Corps had a defined internal tramway unit, the 2nd Canadian Tramway Company, charged with acquiring, building and maintaining trench tramways, the scope of which gradually extended to embrace quite sophisticated systems of several miles in length, effecting an 'interchange' of traffic with the 'main line' WDLR operations. At least one of the second batch of 20hp Motor Rails ordered by the War Office in 1916, as part of the first major order for light railway equipment, was delivered to the 2nd Canadian CTC.[1]

Figures for January 1918[2] show the Canadian Corps operating 53 miles of 'tramway' track, employing 918 personnel, carrying 1,058 tons daily - and all this on 9lb/yd rail! [3]

Lumbermen answer the call

Equally valuable to the Allied war effort was the Canadian Forestry Corps. Under pre-war conditions, Britain imported the bulk of her timber from Europe. Of the 3,000,000 loads of picked timber imported from the Continent each year, about half came from Russia, and one third from France, Sweden and Norway. The war on the Eastern front cut off the supplies of Russian timber almost immediately, just when the demand for timber escalated. At home, timber was needed for the construction of army huts, barracks and ordnance depots; supplementary Government offices, and for boxes and cases for the forwarding of shells and ammunition. In France it was needed for trench and dugout construction, shoring up shell damaged buildings, and the building of 'corduroy' roads across the muddy terrain. Soon, the shortage of timber became acute, and seriously threatened the war effort.

Up to the end of 1915 the French provided all the Allies' requirements, but it rapidly became clear that they could not keep up with demand. Wood was plentiful in Britain,but few workers were qualified as foresters, and many of these had volunteered for the Army and could not be easily released. In February 1916, Mr Bonar Law, Secretary of State for the Colonies, asked the Canadian

Government to recruit, and send to Britain, a Battalion of lumbermen. The response was immediate. The 224th Forestry Battalion was organised, and the first draft arrived in England on 1st April 1917. Ultimately some 101 Companies were deployed in England, Scotland and France, total manpower in France (including attached officers and men from other Allied armies) being over 18,000 men.

The nucleus of each Company was, of course, trained foresters, but men invalided out of the forces, and those unfit for combatant service, were also employed. This makes the achievements of the Corps all the more impressive. German and Austrian prisoners (under CFC supervision) were also used on forestry work, as were Portuguese units, and a motley collection of Norwegian, Swedish, Dutch, Russian and Greek sailors, marooned in Britain after their ships had been sunk. This heterogenous group gained the quite inaccurate title of "Finns", a hangover from an abortive scheme to import Finnish woodsmen.

Widespread use was made of light railways, mostly of 3ft gauge, in Britain, so when the CFC began to exploit the large tracts of forest in France, light railways were laid down as a matter of routine. Due to the availability of material, these were usually 60cm gauge. Some of them were only short 'portable' lines, used for man or animal haulage of raw timber within the forest. Others were more sophisticated systems serving sawmills and carrying finished timber off to standard gauge railheads. 26 steam locomotives, 2 petrol tractors and 287 trucks were used in CFC operations.

68. A Dick Kerr petrol electric hauls a trainload of shells through the ruined village of Lieven-Agres. This is an unusually well-engineered line and may have been captured from the Germans, who regarded their light railways as more 'permanent.' (Canadian 'official,' CO1860)

69. A challenge no doubt welcomed by the Canadian engineers was the construction of this bridge, built to carry the 60cm gauge line across a series of standard gauge tracks. (Canadian 'official,' CO3592)

Two contemporary reports have survived, describing in some detail the organisation of CFC camps in Scotland. Insofar as similar camps were subsequently constructed in France, the descriptions are of some interest and the first of these is reproduced below:

The Canadians at Knockando

"The members of the Canadian Forestry Corps encamped near Knockando station, after several months preparatory work erecting their sawmill, huts, light railway, cable, footbridge etc., have now got into full working order, and a visit to their encampment is both interesting and instructive. The officers are housed in a bungalow on the north side of the railway overlooking the camp, while the men's sleeping quarters are in the large malt barn at the adjoining distillery. The grain loft above the sleeping room serves as a recreation room, and here are the quarters of the YMCA and a canteen. The men are supplied with books, papers and games, while for music they have the use of a piano and a powerful gramophone.

70. Reference to the transport of wounded has been made in an earlier chapter. Here, Canadian troops are using a typical trench tramway 4-wheel truck to carry a man on a stretcher. These trucks are the later generation version, professionally built for the tramways, and with a steel underframe. (Canadian 'official,' CO1545)

The large sawmill is at the east side of the camp and there is a siding to it from the main line for quick and easy transport of the sleepers etc., which are turned out daily in large numbers. The mill produces about 25,000ft of cut wood daily, and the speed at which the wood is cut is an eye-opener. The large wood which is being cut down is on the Ballindalloch estate on the opposite side of the Spey, and a light railway about two miles long has been constructed for the rapid transit of the cut trees. Small bogies on the line convey the logs to the cable head. This cable, which is two inches in diameter and about 700 yards long with its carriage, conveys the logs by gravitation across the river to the sawmill. The empty carriage is pulled back by an engine on the south side of the river. The carriage can accomplish six journeys within an hour, and over 400 logs are conveyed across daily to be sawn up. The logs are thrown on to the platform and then pulled up by machinery on to the sawing bench. The large circular saw is furnished with moveable teeth, and is much thicker than the Scotch saw, thus producing more sawdust, which is removed by a chain bucket arrangement and emptied into a cart for removal. The cut wood is conveyed along the moveable platform, trimmed by the "edger", marked, and loaded into wagons for sending away, or stacked along the loop line. A powerful engine drives the machinery for the mill, and also supplies the motive power for the electric plant which lights the various buildings in the camp.

Proceeding westwards we come to the blacksmith's shop, where horseshoeing and general blacksmith's work is carried on. A short distance off is a small hospital, containing four beds, which owing to the splendid health of the men, are seldom or ever occupied. Passing the orderly room, in

71. As time went on, and casualties mounted, more comfortable methods of transporting wounded had to be devised. This view shows an Ambulance car, locally constructed in Canadian workshops, being inspected by C G Cassels and C Cambie of the Canadian Red Cross. (Canadian 'official,' CO2431)

front of which is a large flagstaff displaying the flag of the maple leaf, we come to the men's messhouse and cookhouse and here the wants of the inner man are well looked after. The cooking is done in a large oven capable of doing a 70lb roast, and in large boiling pans. Each man is supplied with 5lbs of beef weekly, and with potatoes, beans, and mashed turnips he receives an ample dinner to keep him in form for his arduous outdoor work; the man gets three substantial meals daily.

Proceeding across the high swing footbridge which spans the river, and is used by the men going about their work, we have to climb a very steep hill to reach the top. Here are the head of the light railway and the south end of the cable, while close by is the large stable, for the housing of the many horses employed in pulling trees to the side of the line and the pulling of bogies on the railway. Two large sleeping huts have been erected here for the accommodation of about 150 Finns who are expected soon to work in the "bush". The tree fellers are experts at their work, and they soon knock down a tree and knock off its branches, and saw them to the required length" [4]

A further contemporary account gives some interesting statistics about the output of one Scottish camp, and compliments the CFC on its standard of organisation:

72. In contrast to the earlier photo of Baldwin locomotives being delivered via a sleeper ramp, the Canadian railwaymen are demonstrating the effectiveness of their gantry for unloading a new Dick Kerr PE from a standard gauge flat wagon. The track below the gantry is dual gauge, 4ft 8½in and 60cm. The pristine 20hp Simplex (right) shows the contrast in size between the two types of petrol loco.
(Canadian 'official,' CO3806)

73. The “Mechanical Bug,” a locomotive – or more properly an inspection car – constructed by Canadian officers. The “Bug” incorporates the engine from a motorcycle, the flywheel from a sugar refinery, and the belt from a minehead smashed by shellfire.
(Canadian ‘official,’ CO2779)

74. A view on the forestry railway in the Basse Forêt d'Eu, 26th January 1918. The locomotive is a four-coupled 10hp petrol machine, built by Baguley Cars (Burton on Trent). These locomotives had been intended for use on the trench tramways, but were soon relegated to rear areas as their glowing exhaust pipe made them a perfect target! They were however well suited to the lightly laid track on the forestry railways. The locally constructed wagons look crude, but are highly effective for transporting both cut and raw timber.
(Imperial War Museum, Q10255)

75. Most of the railways used by the Canadian Forestry Corps were operated by man or horse power. In this animated scene on the Haute Forêt D'Eu system, operated by the No. 50 POW Company, a horse hauls a four wheel truck carrying a heavy log up onto a transhipment platform. From here it will be rolled onto a motor lorry for transport to a sawmill. (Imperial War Museum, Q10213)

76. Forest railroading at its most primitive – a 'pole' railway constructed by laying timber baulks straight on the ground. Double flanged wheels help to keep the wagon on the rails, despite the wide fluctuations of gauge. (Moray and Elgin Libraries)

The Camp in Abernethy Forest - Canadians at Work

"The 110th Company of the Canadian Forestry Corps was engaged at the Sluggan during the winter of 1916-17 and during most of 1917. On October 15 1917 it sent an advance party to Nethy Forest to prepare the camp there, and as soon as the huts were ready the whole Company followed. This was in December. The huts are built of wooden framing, lined with wood and covered with tar paper, and roofed with rubbered or waterproofed felt. A gravitation water supply has been installed and runs through the camp. The strictest watch is kept over sanitation in all the forestry camps. There is a laundry and in addition to the ordinary washing sheds, there is a bathhouse with hot sprays. There is a hospital hut and dispensary with a CAMC sergeant in charge. No tins or other refuse are allowed to lie about the camp. This is one of the results of the Forestry Corps being arranged as a military unit and under military discipline. When the Forestry Companies leave these woods there will be none of the hideous accumulation of tin cans and rubbish which disfigure the usual encampment.

The distance from the mill to the furthest away point of cutting is three miles. About four miles of narrow gauge railway have been laid down in the woods to bring the logs to the mill.

Cutting began on November 14,1917 and the number of trees felled to the end of September is 52,291. The number of logs is 107,897. This means that on average each tree felled has given an average two saw logs each twelve feet or so in length. The top of the stem too small for sawing makes a pit prop. The amount of lumber sawn at the mill is 4,218,231 f.b.m., and of this there has been shipped 1,178,579 f.b.m., the balance being stacked by the mill. To the total amount of 4,218,231 f.b.m. there should be added 30,000 pieces of pitwood." [5]

[1] *see "Narrow Gauge at War", illus. 29.*

[2] *quoted in "Light Railways of the First World War"*

[3] *Further information, and photographs, will be found in "The Kerry Tramway and other Timber Light Railways" by D Cox and C Krupa (Plateway Press, 1992).*

[4] *"The Northern Scot," 18 May 1918.*

[5] *"Strathspey Herald," 7 November 1918.*

77. A more permanent narrow gauge line, typical of those built by the CFC at numerous locations in Scotland and France. The track appears to be dual gauge, 2ft and 3ft.
(Moray and Elgin Libraries)

Chapter 5

RAILROADERS ANSWER THE CALL

The US Army 12th Engineers Regiment in France, 1917-18.

THE UNITED STATES HAD ONLY A SMALL STANDING ARMY when it declared war in April 1917. A massive recruiting programme was put in hand, and there was no shortage of volunteers. Fighting men were of course the priority, but having studied the experiences of the other protagonists, the American High Command ensured that an efficient logistical operation was in place to back up the front line troops. It is estimated that some 69,000 of the American troops serving abroad were in the military railway service. In November 1918, 13,650 of them were employed on the light railways operated by the American forces.

78. US troops are trained in the essentials of light railway maintenance at Boisleux-au-Mont. In this 2nd September 1917 photo, one of the first known views of US troops on active service, soldiers adjust a block and tackle while a Baldwin 4-6-0T (with its side tank removed) awaits attention in the background.
(US National Archives)

79. Pending the arrival of their own locomotives and rolling stock, US units in France had to train using British equipment. This view shows Baldwin 4-6-0T No. 780, built for the WDLR in December 1916, with American troops and two British Army personnel present. Note the tongue-in-cheek sign "Royal Mail" on the first wagon.
(Museum of Army Transport)

Four US regiments were responsible for construction or operation of light railways; the 12th, 14th, 21st and 22nd Engineers. All were volunteers and the bulk of them were drawn from the ranks of the US standard gauge railroads. Evidence suggests that the 'culture shock' of being employed on the toy-like 60cm gauge railroads was as great for these men as it had been for their British and Dominion predecessors! But, like them, the US railwaymen soon adapted to the different operating methods and disciplines needed on the two-foot gauge.

The US 12th Engineers Regiment arrived in England on August 12th, 1917 and (along with three other Engineer regiments) marched through London on August 15th, to an ecstatic welcome by the war weary British population. US forces still being thin on the ground in France at this time, the 12th were ordered to the British Front. The regiment's Official History takes up the story...

"In less than a month from the time of entraining at Camp Gaillard, St. Louis, and within 12 months of mobilization, the 12th found itself on foreign soil in the shell-torn valley of the Somme, under direct shell fire of the German batteries. Here it was, on the Somme, that the regiment later became, in the verbiage of the Britisher, "the Twelfth American Royal Engineers." This designation which bespeaks the warm friendship and high regard which sprung up between soldiers of the two countries, will always remain a matter of pride with the Twelfth.

First experiences of Light Railway working

The narrow gauge roads that were to be operated by the regiment were the light railways of the British Army. Most of the track was sectional, sixteen pound rails, sixteen feet long and held to gauge by four or five pressed steel ties to the section. The gauge was 60cm - practically two feet. The track was not used for heavy power until further supported by wooden ties jumped between the steel ones. The ballast was of various types - some cinder, some broken brick from ruins, but for the larger part, chalk, which was characteristic of this part of the country. The chalk, however, was too soft for a satisfactory ballast, and after a freeze went to pieces rapidly, requiring a great deal of work in maintenance. The minimum curvature was a thirty meter radius, and super elevation from one half inch to one inch.

On August 31st, Capt. Phillips, with men from Companies C, D, E and F, was given the first section of railroad taken over for operation and maintenance. This was the DZ (pronounced De Zed) Line from Montigny to Vermand, 3.81 miles in length. Four days later this territory was extended to include the Roisel yard, and Sept. 26th the Harcourt branch of the DZ lines. Captain Green, with Company A, on September 27th, took over the operation of the Fins-Heudecourt and the lines from Fins to AX129, both branches of the AX lines, as well as the entire system known as the "AX extension lines". At the close of September the Regiment was operating thirty-nine miles of track, maintaining twenty miles, had graded two miles and laid 1.3 miles of new track, and had ballasted 2 miles of both new and old track. The total tonnage for the month was 107,472, while locomotive mileage was 5,309.

October found the regiment in full swing on the operation and maintenance of light railways extending from Cambrai to St. Quentin on the British Third Army Front. The men were rapidly becoming accustomed to the peculiar conditions under which the railways were operated. At first it was hard to regulate the use of lanterns and lights in the more advanced positions, especially as the bulk of the work had to be done at night; but a few timely reminders in the form of German shells emphasised the necessity of being careful.

80. A posed view with a different Baldwin 4-6-0T at a typical light railway depot. The locally constructed water tower (left) is yet another variation on a theme. (Museum of Army Transport)

81. A train consisting of four 'empties' plus two 'fulls' (one dangerously so!), poses on a typical girder bridge, built by Army engineers to take the 60cm gauge line across a declivity and minor road. Army engineers were trained to erect bridges like this in a short space of time – perhaps as little as a day – provided sufficient materials were available. (Museum of Army Transport)

Several despatching systems were tried, and the method which proved most satisfactory developed from the "train sheet, written order" system. Due to the inadequacy of the paper supply the verbal order took the place of the written order. The results obtained by this method proved its superiority over that used previously by the British on these lines.

The car (wagon) situation was always acute. There were always more orders for cars than there were cars available. Finally, to remedy this situation, a four hour demurrage system was put into operation, and then most of the equipment made at least two trips daily.

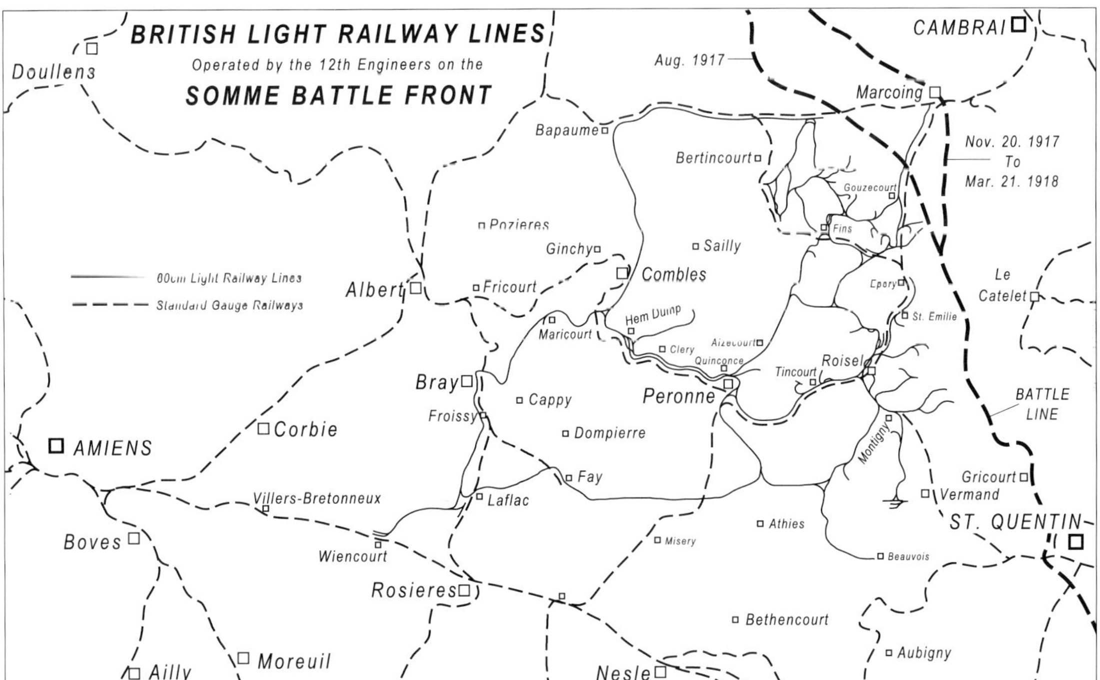

82. A four engine 'meet' at a marshalling yard somewhere in France. British Westinghouse PE No. 2006 can be identified, but not the three Baldwins. (Museum of Army Transport)

Light Railways under fire

In October 1917, preparations were started for the great offensive against Cambrai. Enormous quantities of ammunition, barbed wire, "duck boards" and army material of every description was moved from Roisel, Tincourt and Fins broad gauge railheads to the front by light railways. Early in November the growing light railway tonnage made it necessary to extend the working radius of locomotives. Men and officers remained on duty from 15 to 18 hours a day, giving their best efforts to insure a successful outcome to the approaching action. During the latter part of the month ground mists and low visibility aided the light railway program in making it possible to operate steam power closer to the front line trenches.

Within a few days' time after General Byng's successful drive, the light railways were connected across what had been "No Man's Land" to the German Light Railway system[1]. This work was done by the Canadians, the connection being made at Marcoing. Conditions had just about gotten back to normal and trench warfare resumed when the enemy launched his counter-offensive. Early in the morning of November 30th, his artillery opened up on the British positions. Shells fell in both the Tincourt and Fins camps. By noon the enemy had taken Gouzeaucourt and advanced to a point between there and Fins. Information about the enemy's progress had not yet reached the American and Canadian engineers, when suddenly they came face to face with the gray uniforms of the oncoming Germans. Thus it was that the first Americans fought in the world war.[2] Caught without arms, they fought with whatever they had at hand, where possible, picking up a fallen British comrade's rifle, or getting one from a dead Hun.

There was only one casualty in the Twelfth; Private Fritz Fulks was wounded by a German machine gun while trying to save one of the light railway trains caught in the advance. Of the train crews that were operating in and about Gouzeaucourt, some managed to get their trains out of the area. The detachment at the advance tractor sheds east of Fins had to evacuate hurriedly with all equipment, but were able to return when the tanks had cleared Gouzeaucourt.

The light railway work began to ease up after the Cambrai offensive, and attention was turned to the construction of new lines leading to the rear, looking forward to the day when the great German drive would come.

83. By 1918 the US Army had in place a well organised light railway training programme, with 60cm gauge lines laid down at a number or camps across the United States. A Baldwin 'gas mechanical' poses at the Trench Railroad Camp, Humphreys, Virginia, in 1918.
(Author's collection)

A hard winter on the Somme

It was deemed advisable, on account of the increased aerial and artillery activity around Fins, to move the bulk of "A" Company and their locomotives further south. This was effected about December 7th, and the main body moved to Quinconce, near Peronne. The first snow fell about the middle of December, and remained on the ground for over a month. The weather grew much colder, and the daily 1 lb coal ration per man did not go very far towards comfort. The snow drifted so deep on the roads that all motor transport was stopped, and the burden of traffic was thrown on the light railways. It was only by tremendous efforts in removing drifts that many of the lines through cuts were kept open.

Christmas, 1917, is one that will long be remembered. Each camp had its Christmas Eve celebration, but that held in the round house at Montigny was probably the most unique. Captain Foster, then O.C. DZ lines, cleared out the roundhouse except for one Baldwin locomotive which was used to run a generator for lighting power. A cedar tree was duly salvaged, mounted over the pit and strung with electric lights, home made ornaments and socks filled with popcorn. When all was ready the Twelfth and their friends, the British, were invited into the entertainment which featured music by the Irish pipers, eats, and an announcement by the commanding officer of 'no reveille' the next morning. The 'bully beef' and tea menu the next day was varied by two truck loads of turkey with the accessories which Lieutenant Johnson obtained at Nevers.

Working conditions became increasingly difficult due to the frequency of the enemy's bombing raids and his well directed artillery fire which was continually wrecking track and equipment. Fins and Quinconce were bombed December 23rd. In an air raid on Montigny January 28th, the DZ control was damaged and fourteen casualties resulted. During a daylight raid February 19th, an anti-aircraft shell which failed to explode in the air entered the round-house at Montigny, and exploded on hitting a rail; two men were wounded.

Train wreck at Montigny

The first death in the Regiment occurred December 22nd, when Private Aubuchon of Company "F" was killed in a wreck at CY 16 near Leiramont. The first serious wreck occurred on January 15th,

Above: 84. From late 1917 onwards the US army received its own purpose-built equipment. Learning from British and French experience, the 2-6-2T wheel arrangement was made standard. This works official photo shows the first of 195 Baldwin 2-6-2T's built for the US forces between September and December 1917.

Below: 85. Like their contemporary WDLR designs the US Army Baldwins were equipped with hoses to facilitate watering from streams, ditches and shell holes.
(both – collection John Agnew)

86. The bulk of the US Army's motive power in France consisted of 'gas mechanical' (petrol mechanical) 0-4-0's. Powerful and reliable, they nevertheless displayed the occasional malfunction when in service, as depicted in this view near Void in 1918. No. 7023 is a 50hp example, of which 189 were delivered.
(US National Archives, courtesy John Agnew)

when a DZ engine and train left the track on the Vernand line near Montigny Sugar Mill. This resulted in the death of two British soldiers and slight injuries to eight others.A subsequent enquiry held by British officers established that the accident was unavoidable, and due to the inability of the engineer to control the train on the steep grade with slippery rails.

On 28th February the Regiment came under the control of the British Fifth Army (North), of which Colonel I R Collins was A D L R. Although sceptical at first of Americans, Col. Collins later expressed the opinion that the Twelfth was the most efficient railroad organisation he had known during his experience with the Allied Armies.

The German offensive - March 1918

The enemy barrage broke forth at 4.30 Thursday morning, March 21st; the long expected battle had begun.At 9.00 p.m. orders from A D L R started the evacuation of all power and rolling stock on the DZ lines back to Hancourt, and the movement of companies "C" and "E" to Le Mesnil. These movements and the supply of ammunition to batteries along the rail lines consumed the entire night. Maintenance parties, working with a company of the 12th Canadian Railway Troops, repaired breaks caused by shell fire, throughout the 21st, allowing ration and ammunition trains to be handled.

During the night of the 21st, the Tincourt crews salvaged 9 cars of eighteen pounders from the CY 9 ammunition dump, which was then burning as a result of artillery fire, and 26 cars from CY103

8007

Above: 89. Where military 'duties' permitted, the kind-hearted US troops would allow their railways to be used for humanitarian purposes. Civilian refugees and their worldly possessions – including goats – are transported to safety on an improvised train at Bouillonville (Meuse) on September 20th 1918.

Page opposite – Upper: 87. The US Army made thrifty use of captured German petrol locos, often allocating them running numbers in the 78xx series. When US equipment arrived in quantity, the captured locos were stored, as in this view, probably taken at Sourcy.

Lower: 88. Supplementing the Canadian Army's logging operation in France were no less than 18,000 American Forestry troops. The 20th Engineers built a 14 mile long 60cm gauge line at Eclairon, in the Vosges mountains, where 35hp Baldwin gas mechanical No. 8007 is seen at work on July 8th, 1918.

(All – US National Archives, courtesy John Agnew)

LIGHT RAILWAY MILEAGE AND TONNAGE - 12th ENGINEERS

Month	Miles of line in operation	Track laid (miles)	Ton-miles operated	Locomotive mileage
Sept 1917	39	1.3	107,472	5,309
Oct 1917	41	-	264,163	8,394
Nov 1917	64.2		303,065	15,270
Dec 1917	77.3	0.5	295,136	20,223
Jan 1918	77.3		293,268	18,646
Feb 1918	85		396,163	20,530
Mar 1918	N/A	N/A	N/A	N/A

dump, east of Roisel. In the evening of the 21st, the evacuation of Fins was ordered. Further retreats were ordered, and eventually the Regiment - with most of its equipment still intact - was reassembled at La Flaque and Weincourt.

On orders being received to retreat further to Vequemont, rear guards were left at La Flaque and Weincourt. When it was apparent that the latter was about to fall to the enemy, orders were issued by the A D L R to strip the locomotives of injectors and side rods, and the tractors of magnetos and compressors. This was done, and the parts buried."

For the next four months, the regiment was engaged in the construction of a standard gauge railroad, outside the terms of this treatise. The "History" describes this work, and the eventual detachment of the Regiment from the BEF, and their move south for duty on the American Front. The Historian concludes:- "It was with a feeling of general regret that the Twelfth left the British Front. Relations that had existed between the Regiment and the British with whom it served for a year, were always the most cordial. The Regiment in leaving carried with it the most profound respect and admiration for the wonderful organisation, discipline and bulldog courage of the British Army."

[1] *The German "Feldbahnen" were, of course, also 60cm gauge, and the inter-availability of equipment was a useful facility exploited by all sides in the conflict!*

[2] *This is not strictly true. American artillery had been in action, on a southern sector of the Western Front, a few weeks before, on October 23rd.*

90. Eighty 2-6-2T's built by Davenports, virtually identical to the Baldwin 2-6-2T's, were delivered too late for active service and most were deployed on training camps in the USA. No. 5268 was built in May 1919 and spent its life at Camp (Fort) Benning, near Columbus, Ohio.
(collection – John Agnew)

Chapter Six

BEHIND THE LINES IN THE ALTO ADIGE

Light Railways on the Italian Front.

ITALY FOUGHT ON THE SIDE OF THE ALLIES in World War 1 and, although the scale of combat was unimpressive in relation to other spheres of the war, the Italian Army tied down considerable numbers of Austrian and German troops that would otherwise have been deployed against the Allied armies elsewhere.

In 1917, with the Allies on the offensive on most battle fronts, support for the war was waning in Austro-Hungary, and large elements of its ethnically-mixed Army had become unreliable. To present the Austrians with a morale-boosting victory, the Central Powers supreme commander, First Quartermaster-General Ludendorff, ordered an attack on the extreme eastern quarter of the front, at Caporetto. Six German and nine Austrian Divisions took part in the attack which achieved almost complete surprise, and forced the Italians back, first to defensive positions on the river Taglimento, and then, in November 1917, to the river Piave. Here the battered Italian forces were shored up by British and French reinforcements. The line stabilised and in the event the British forces saw little action.

Light Railway Development

The British units sent in to bolster the Italian defence were fresh from the Ypres front, where the value of light railways had already been convincingly displayed. On January 8th 1918 it was decided that a Light Railways HQ staff and one Light Railway Operating Company should be sent out, together with a supply of 60cm gauge track and suitable locomotives and rolling stock. Orders were

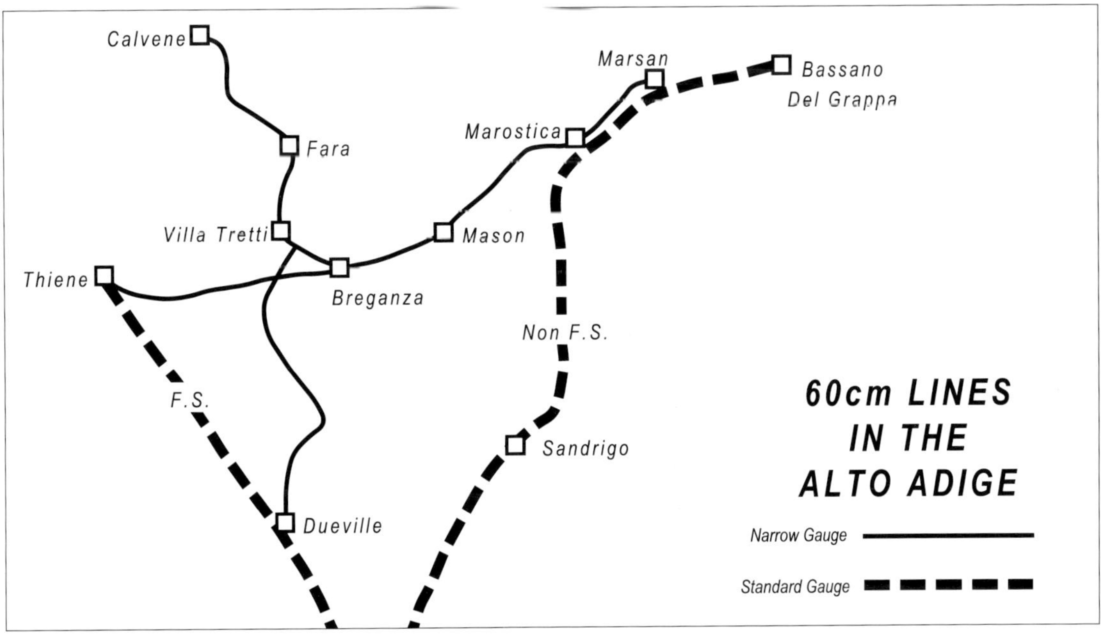

90. Following the proven success of the Hunslet 4-6-0T's in France, 80 more were ordered for service in Italy and the Middle East, but only the first 16 reached Italy before hostilities ceased. This view shows some of the initial batch on the dockside at Barry awaiting despatch.
(Collection – F Jones)

92. The Motor Rails were used in supply roles, some way behind the front line. Here, British officers, other ranks and Italian civilian workers demonstrate the carrying capacity of a train comprising three 'D' class wagons.
(Imperial War Museum, Q26163)

placed for 40 Hunslet 4-6-0T's, but in the event only 16 were recorded as being delivered to Italy. 15 'tractors', 240 wagons and 40 miles of track were also delivered. The LROC personnel were employed in working British traffic over the Thiene - Calvene Light Railway. This was one of a network of 60cm gauge railways in the Brenta sector, about which little is known. The accompanying map shows the extent of known lines. The principal function of the 60cm gauge lines laid down by the LROC seems to have been the ferrying of supplies, and the transport of civilian workers employed by the British forces, using the Simplex locomotives.

Fate of the Hunslet 4-6-0T's

Following the end of the war, the glut of surplus light railway material on the market made it uneconomical to ship the steam locomotives back to Britain. It is probable that most were scrapped locally. However unpublished research by Edoardo Tonarelli has established that a quantity of them were purchased by dealers Glauco Greco of Reggio Emilia. The company had their own workshops and are known to have purchased many ex-Austrian and Italian military locomotives for resale. Disposal of three of the Hunslet 4-6-0T's has been confirmed:-

HE1308 (WDLR 2336) - regauged to 750mm and acquired by the Bari-Barletta Tramway circa 1928. Became line's No. 12, and was scrapped late 1940's or early 1950's.

HE1298 (WDLR 2326) and HE1303 (WDLR2333) - to Bacu Abis (Sardinia) lignite colliery (60cm gauge) in early 1920's. Disposal dates unknown.

Italian Propaganda posters.

Chapter 7

LINES OF COMMUNICATION IN THE BALKANS

from the "Railway Gazette" Special War Transportation Number, September 21, 1920. Reprinted by Courtesy of Railway Gazette International.

WITH THE OBJECT OF AFFORDING AID TO SERBIA, which was being invaded by the Austrian and Bulgarian armies, French and British forces in October, 1915, commenced to land at Salonica. The 10th Division of the British Army was brought over from the Dardanelles, its orders being to establish itself for the winter in Salonica and not to cross the Greek frontier unless this was violated.

A decision, however, was reached that the French should push up into Serbia with the object of relieving the Serbs, who were then being hardly pressed by the Austrian and Bulgarian invaders, and General Mahon, commanding the 10th Division, received orders from London to advance as far as

93. This view of a supply dump near Stavros provides a stark picture of the desolate landscape typical of this part of Greece. Although 'line' work on the two routes radiating from Stavros was carried out by steam traction, an unknown number of 40hp Simplexes were supplied for local work. LR2257 is a standard 'protected' type, identical to those used on the Western Front. (Imperial War Museum, Q15137)

Lake Doiran, just across the Greek frontier. Here he relieved the French, who were holding the right wing of the Allied front, and protected the line of communication of the main French force which had advanced and become engaged with the enemy up the Vardar, 80 miles from Salonica. Unfortunately, however, the Allies arrived too late in Salonica to stop the retirement of the Serbian army, who were outnumbered and overwhelmed by the Austrians from the north and the Bulgars from the east.

In consequence, after a bold but ineffective attempt to save at least the southern part of Serbia, the Allied Army had to fall back to a line running along the Greek frontier from Vodena through Doiran and following the River Struma to the Gulf of Orfano in the Aegean Sea. The army was thus thrown solely upon its own resources, and, far from receiving help from the Greeks, had to look upon them as a constant menace from all sides. It had to import from a base thousands of miles away and improvise in a barren country all the requirements needed for the maintenance in proper fettle of an enormous number of men and for the carrying out of modern warfare. Villages were scattered, primitive and thinly populated, the roads were mostly mere tracks, and although three railways were in existence, these ran at divergent angles and necessitated considerable extra construction and improvement. The Allies, therefore, had to build up slowly and laboriously the main part of the system of locomotion necessary for the movement of troops and supplies by the erection of piers and bridges and the construction of miles of road and railway track.

94. Construction of the Stavros – Sarakli line was a massive undertaking, involving many embankments, cuttings and trestle bridges. Only the help of 4,000 Turkish prisoners of war enabled the railway to be built in six months. The line was laid out to full 'light railway' standards, with permanent stations, passing loops etc. This is Planica station in 1918.
(Imperial War Museum, Q15147)

Light Railway Developments

The British front line originally ran along the River Struma, which enters the Gulf of Rendina at Chai Aghizi. The British occupied the ground on the west bank of the mouth of the Struma and a very small piece of ground on the east bank. Supplies were landed by lighters at Tasli, a few kilometres south west of Chai Aghizi, the lighters being run there from Stavros in the south-west corner of the Gulf. It was frequently impossible to land at Tasli, and the Navy could not allow supply ships to go to this part of the coast. On the other hand, Stavros Bay was protected from attack by submarine, and it was generally possible to land supplies there, a small pier having been constructed.

Originally, there was no rail communication whatever between Salonica and Stavros and, apart from the sea, there were no means of getting there except by a track through the hills; this route was quite unsuitable for motor lorries, so men and stores had to be sent there by small steamer from Salonica. In January, 1917, consideration was given to the possibility of sending large vessels to Stavros to relieve the congestion at Salonica itself and avoid superfluous handling of goods, and a suggestion for extra piers and lighters was approved.

95. This view of Baldwin 4-6-0T No. 973 and an unidentified Henschel 0-4-0T could have been taken on either the Stavros or Snevce system. Nothing is known of the Henschel, but it may have been acquired locally within Greece.
(Imperial War Museum, Q15136)

The Stavros-Tasli Light Railway

In 1916 the British had constructed a 60cm line for 15km from Stavros towards Tasli, and by the end of the year the formation was nearly complete for extending it to that place. It was then proposed to run a double 60cm line from Stavros past Tasli to Chai Aghizi and on a formation suitable for a standard gauge railway, the reasons for not making this a standard gauge line in the first instance being (1) the difficulty of landing S.G. rolling-stock at Stavros; (2) the doubt as to whether S.G. material and rolling stock could be supplied; and (3) the necessity for completing the line in time for operations before the hot weather. If necessary, the provision of a standard gauge line could be commenced at any time without interfering with the use of the 60cm line as soon as material could be supplied, the 60cm track and rolling-stock being then taken up and used for other purposes of the army.

The ultimate aim of the Chai Aghizi line was to enable the concentration of troops on the west bank of the Struma and to follow up the advance, connecting subsequently with the main Seres line. For this, there were two alternatives: -

(1) To cross the Struma near its mouth and join the main J.S.C.[1] line between Borna and Angista; or
(2) To keep to the west side of the lake of Tahinos, the north-west part of which is dry, and join up probably west of Seres.

The advantage of the first scheme was a shorter railway, the disadvantages steeper gradients, bridging of the Struma and several tunnels and cuttings. From a railway point of view, the second scheme seemed preferable, as from a preliminary survey it was found that the gradients need not

96. Snevce, terminus of the line from Sarigol, showing the original French lightweight (9.5kg/m) track and Decauville motive power. Later, the line was relaid to heavier standards by the British Army, and Baldwin 4-6-0T's introduced.
(Imperial War Museum, Q15121)

97. British Army engineers constructing a pile bridge over the Galiko river, to carry the the Gramatna–Rajnova 60cm gauge line, during the winter of 1917-18. Note the steam driven pile driver. (Imperial War Museum, Q15142)

exceed 1 in 100. If constructed, it would be a much better means of supplying the forces on the Struma front than by the existing Seres Road, and whether the advance was through the Rupel Pass or towards Drama, it would be distinctly superior to the J.S.C. line through Doiran to Demir Hissar. The extension of the line would mean the supply of 66 miles of track with points and crossings and at least seven additional six-coupled engines and 240 wagons, whilst for operation east of Seres, one locomotive would have to be supplied for each 15 miles operated conditional on the advance. It was realised, however, that the Struma Valley was nothing more nor less than a malarial swamp, and the railway would have to go right through it, causing a heavy drain on personnel.

By the middle of February, 1917, a single 60cm line of 16lb material had been laid from Stavros to Chai Aghizi; in the meantime, a quantity of 2ft 6in gauge material was being converted in Egypt to 60cm, 10 miles of which was on its way to Salonica. In its existing state the capacity of the line was very small, and owing also to lack of engines, the traffic was limited to 150 tons a day.

98. Ekaterini–Dranista Light Railway: this was the last 60cm gauge line constructed in Salonica, and served lignite mines at Dranista. Turkish POW's were again used as labour for the construction work, and are shown here excavating a cutting. (Imperial War Museum, Q15158)

It was then decided to defer the relaying of the line from Stavros and its extension along Lake Tahinos for consideration only in the event of an advance, though it was pointed out that irrespective of an advance, the proposal had an economic value attached to it, for at the time 600 lorries, excluding ambulances, were being utilised daily to supply three divisions and one mounted brigade on the Struma front. As each of these lorries required two drivers, there were at least 1,000 men engaged on the service in addition to guards and officers and repairing staff. In addition, the constant use of this road involved a very large expenditure on repairs, the weekly percentage of breakages of front springs, for instance, being 24 per cent., and even after the expenditure of considerable time and money, it would not be possible to render the Seres Road suitable for motor transport. Exclusive of ammunition, which varied up to a maximum of 300 tons a day, 750 tons of stores and supplies were being moved daily by the road, and it was estimated that a standard gauge railway from Stavros to the Struma would give much greater efficiency with eight locomotives and not more than 120 men for operation and 100 for maintenance. Sixty-centimetre gauge was not recommended owing to the fact that the line would be about 100km in length, and also that standard gauge would only require for the same work about one-sixth of the locomotive staff and one third of the traffic and maintenance staff, and would be more reliable and easy to maintain.

In March it was found impossible to carry on the work within a distance of 4km from the mouth of the Struma, owing to fire from enemy batteries, but the laying of the single track into Tasli was completed by the middle of May after some delay awaiting material. In the meantime the main strength of the British forces had been moved to the western sector of the line for the advance at Doiran, and at the end of the spring campaigning season it was decided to move the British troops back from the malarial Struma Valley to prevent, if possible, the heavy sick list of the previous year. Consequently, the main forces were withdrawn to the hills, outposts only being left at fortified bridgeheads, and the proposed extension of the Tasli line was not proceeded with.

The Guvesne to Stavros Light Railway

Attention was next drawn to the possibility of connecting Salonica with Stavros by rail. A direct connection in an easterly direction from Salonica was not possible owing to the big range of hills between there and Lake Langaza, and it was deemed advisable to follow the line of least resistance

99. The official caption for this photo is "Decauville engine with shot holes being repaired" and claims the location is Gallipoli. However no locomotive worked railways have been recorded on the Gallipoli front, so the location is almost certainly Salonica. The view may date from the period (mentioned above) when some ex-French Army lines were operated by British and Dominion troops.
(Imperial War Museum, Q32180)

by using, for the commencement, the already existing Arakli branch of the Guvesne standard gauge line, and running thence along the southern banks of Lakes Langaza and Beshik into Stavros. This and the Tasli line would enable supplies for the army on the Struma to be conveyed by land, and would obviate water transport in a sea infested by enemy submarines, whilst also the Admiralty were anxious that the use of Stavros as a harbour should be discontinued if possible owing to the submarine danger. Accordingly, in October, 1917, a survey was commenced for a 60cm single line from Arakli. By the commencement of the following month, 20km had been laid, but the question was then raised as to the advisability of continuing the work owing to the probable small quantity of traffic likely to be dealt with. At that time, however, it was possible in certain circumstances that the army might have to withdraw to a more retired line covering Salonica, in which event a railway such as that proposed would be useful for the feeding of the troops, supplies being taken from railhead by mountain tracks north of Beshik and Langaza Lakes. The railway was, therefore, proceeded with and opened for traffic on April 1, 1918. An R.O.D. Company was formed locally for the operation of the line - 93km in length.

Fortunately, events did not necessitate the withdrawal of the troops from the forward positions they occupied, but the traffic passing over the line soon justified its construction - in fact, it came to be the most important light railway in the Salonica theatre of war. During the quarter ending December, 1918, out of the 3,000 tons a week carried on the light railways, the Stavros line was responsible for 2,500 and employed much the greater part of the rolling-stock. As a consequence of

100. A fire at a British Army dump in Salonica (its precise location not identified) in June 1916. As the fire spreads, troops load supplies onto a hastily assembled train, headed by a Decauville 0-6-0T, before the flames reach them.
(Imperial War Museum, Q32120)

the opening of the line, traffic by sea into Stavros rapidly declined, and ceased altogether in the middle of September, 1918.

The Sarigol to Snevce Light Railway

Running in a northerly direction from Barigol on the J.S.C. Railway is a 60cm line to a place called Snevce, 28km away, situated at the foot of the Krusha Balkan Mountains, along which ran our front line. Up to the end of November, 1916, this was worked by the French to supply an Italian division, but about this time a British division took over, and the line and rolling-stock were handed over to us. In the following June a survey was made for the purpose of re-aligning and re-laying the railway with 33-lb. track, and the work was completed by the end of October.

By this time a 60cm line was being constructed from a junction with the Snevce line at Gramatna to Rajanovo via Kushova, the object of this line being to facilitate the conveyance of supplies to the troops on the Krusha Range. From Kushova two extensions were to run to Lelovo and Hozo Mah respectively, though these apparently were not proceeded with. The Gramatna-Rajanovo line was commenced on September 24, 1917, and was completed and open for traffic by February 1, 1918. In the meantime, the Snevce Railway was being extended to Karamudli to obviate a certain amount of road transport, sidings being laid and a large depot opened there. The extension was completed in February, 1918.

The length of the Sarigol-Snevce-Gramatna Railways was about 66km, and although only single track 60cm, they were worked with high capacity wagons and engines. They were the means of supplying the troops on the Krusha Hills and thus saving an enormous amount of road transport over difficult country; in fact, the troops relied on this railway solely for their existence, as there were no roads between Sarigol and the front line. In the early days, subsequent to our taking over from the French, there were repeated wash-outs, and the situation often became critical, but this trouble ceased as soon as the re-laying and re-alignment of the track had been completed.

Other light railways in Macedonia were the Janesh–Gugunchi, supplying a British brigade and re-laid in the spring of 1918, and the Spancova–Oreovica, which was handed over to us by the French, and another important light railway was the Ekaterini–Dranista line in Greece.

The Ekaterini-Dranista Light Railway

Ekaterini is situated on the western shore of the Gulf of Salonica, and is one of the principal stations on the northern section of the Plati–Athens Railway. It figures largely in the Salonica operations. In December, 1916, following on trouble in Athens, when a detachment of French sailors were treacherously fired upon, the Allies feared an advance by Greek Royalist troops into Thessaly and to the rear of the French line of communication with Monastir. To stop the advance towards Salonica along the coast, two infantry brigades and some artillery were sent by the British to Ekaterini at the foot of Mount Olympus to bar the passage; consequently, it became necessary to work supply trains to Ekaterini via Plati, but, owing to heavy rains, wash outs occurred on December 8, 9 and 10, causing 16 breaches in the line over a distance of 30km Labour was accordingly withdrawn from other parts of the theatre of war, and the line was repaired through to Ekaterini by December 15, when the working was handed over to the French.

Owing to the shortage of coal for the use of the armies in Salonica, it became necessary to seek fresh supplies of fuel. Lignite mines were known to exist in the hills at Dranista, and in February, 1918, a survey was commenced for a 60cm branch to run from the Plati–Athens line at Ekaterini into the hills at Dranista, 27km away, to enable lignite to be readily brought down to the main line and, if necessary, to the seaport for shipment to Egypt, &c. This line was completed and opened for traffic on September 1, 1918.

[1] *Jonction Salonique Constantinople*

101. Mentioned only in passing in the "Railway Gazette" is the line from Janesh (Yanesh) to Kalinova. This was constructed by the British 26th Division (who were not railway troops) and was also worked by them. The line proved its worth during the winter of 1916-17 when roads in the area were impassable, and the Kilinder lateral was under constant enemy fire. Consequently the line was the only means of supply for the British brigade holding this section of the front. It is believed that Hudson 0-6-0WT's worked this line later, but in this October 1916 view a Decauville 0-6-0T provides the motive power, and four-wheel wagons the somewhat basic accommodation.
(Lt. Col. C Wheeler)

102. A short 60cm gauge line was built by the British Army from an advanced depot at Likovan to Mirova, late in 1916. Its purpose was to supply British forces in the Struma valley. The line is recorded as being worked by horse and mule power, and this view is almost certainly of this line. The line was closed in 1918 and the rails lifted for use elsewhere.
(Imperial War Museum, Q32724)

Chapter 8

FROM SUEZ TO THE GATES OF PALESTINE

Light Railways in the Palestine-Arabian campaign.

IN AUGUST 1914 THE OTTOMAN EMPIRE - whose frontiers then embraced not just Turkey but also present-day Lebanon, Syria, Israel, Jordan, Saudi Arabia and parts of Iraq - had remained neutral. But her historic enmity with Russia, and astute courtship by German military and political emissaries, drew her into the conflict on the side of the Central Powers on 27 October 1914. Under the leadership of German officers, the Turkish Army posed a serious threat to the Suez Canal, then a lifeline to much of the British Empire. Turkish plans were in existence as early as August 1914 for an expeditionary force to travel the 1,275 miles from Haidar Pasa to the Canal, using incomplete railway routes (of standard, metre and 1.05cm gauges), with the final 250 miles to be covered on foot.

First Assault on the Canal

The first echelon of the Turkish Expeditionary Force, which totalled 12,642 men, 968 horses, 12,000 camels and 328 oxen, left Beersheba on 14th January 1915. It reached the Canal on 3rd February and the assault, although carried out with great courage, was beaten off by the (mainly) Indian defending troops, backed up by supporting gunfire from French warships.

Despite this, the threat from the Turks remained acute. A three line plan of defence was quickly created by the British, with the first line 11,000 yards east of the Canal, the second line at 6,500 yards, and the final line on the Canal itself. Lieutenant-General Sir Archibald Murray was in command of a motley force known as the EEF (Egyptian Expeditionary Force). It included Indian infantry, British yeomanry, the ANZAC Mounted Division (comprising the 1st, 2nd and 3rd Australian Light Horse Brigades[1] and the New Zealand Mounted Rifle Brigade), and units of the Imperial Camel Corps.

103. An Orenstein & Koppel 0-4-0WT, impressed into British Army service, pictured at Aston Post on one of the 60cm gauge supply lines laid down on the east bank of the Suez Canal. (Imperial War Museum, Q57726)

Role of the Light Railways

Logistics are the key to the efficiency of all armies, and especially those in a largely defensive role. This fundamental point seems to have been appreciated in the Middle East theatre as early as 1915, sometime before it became obvious to tacticians on the Western Front. From Zigazig to Ismailia the standard gauge railway was doubled, roads were extended and improved, ferries supplemented by bridges.

The main sub-standard gauge in use throughout Egypt was 2ft 6in, one 120 mile line from Oasis Junction to El Kharga having been opened in 1907, and during the War a further line of this gauge was constructed for military purposes from a point on the Beni Mazar-Sandafa standard gauge line out towards the Bahria Oasis in the Western Desert. Privately owned lines, mainly serving sugar plantations, also existed. Equipment of this gauge, and the expertise to use it was therefore immediately available, and no time was lost in bringing it into use to assist the defensive works. The Railway Gazette of September 21 1920 records that the Egyptian State Railways undertook to lay eight short 2ft 6in gauge lines on the east bank of the Canal, all of which had to be finished by the middle of January 1916 (this was based on an order from the C in C Egypt dated November 25th, 1915). The State Railways provided 40km of track, the balance coming from a stock of material that had been sent to Alexandria for use at Gallipoli, but not wanted there due to the failure of the Allied assault. Most of the labour for these works was provided by the State Railways, with assistance from two RE Construction Companies, though the men from military sources numbered only about 500 out of a total of some 18,000 employed by the Railway on military works. The maximum extent of the 2ft 6in gauge lines was the second line of defence, this being a distance at which enemy artillery fire became a possible danger.

104. The interchange point between the 2ft 6in gauge line from Ferry Post, and the light 60cm gauge system. The 2ft 6in gauge locomotive, No. 74, is one of a class of twenty three Hawthorn Leslie 0-4-0 55hp petrol locomotives, originally despatched to Alexandria for use at Gallipoli. With the failure of that campaign, the equipment went to Egypt instead. (Australian War Memorial, G1461)

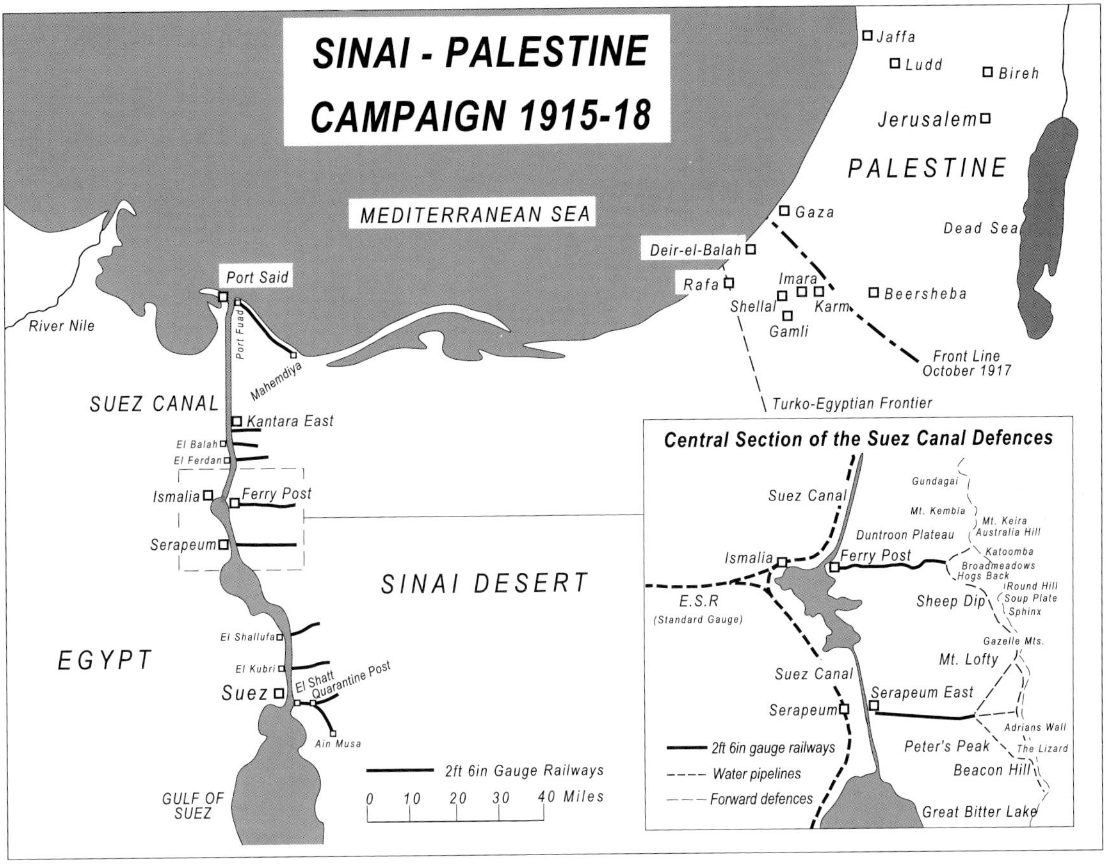

Full details of the 2ft 6in gauge lines remain to be discovered, but preliminary research by Paul Cotterell[2] points to the existence of at least eight systems, and outline details of these are provided on Map 8. A ninth system was proposed at the meeting point of the Great Bitter Lake and Little Bitter Lake, but this line appears not to have been built.

To bridge the gap between the second line of defence and the front line itself, 60cm gauge lines were adopted, for reasons identical to those applying on the Western Front (speed of construction, ease of repair and flexibility in a fluid military situation). Recent research[3] suggests that 60cm gauge lines were laid down in the area east of the Canal as part of the Canal's defensive line from 1915 onwards. These comprise some railways south of Kantara East around a place named Ballybunion, but in addition there were 60cm gauge lines from the rear trenches, where 2ft 6in gauge lines terminated, to the forward trenches. One such line ran east from the railhead connecting with Ferry Post near Ismailia, where in the forward areas there were installations named Gundagai, Mount Kembla, Mount Keira, Broadmeadows, Australia Hill, Katoomba and Sheep Dip! (The names of these locations provide clear evidence of the early involvement of ANZAC units in the operation of the 60cm gauge lines). Other 60cm gauge 'feeder' systems radiated from the eastern ends of the 2ft 6in gauge lines based on El Balah and El Ferdan (to the south of Kantara), and from Serapeum East.

The existence of these 60cm gauge railways predates the 'official' use of this gauge for military purposes, and therefore no equipment was sent out from Great Britain for use at Suez at this stage. All equipment had to be requisitioned from local sources and it is ironical that most of what was available was of German manufacture. Photographs show a variety of 0-4-0WT and 0-4-2WT locomotives from Orenstein and Koppel, Krauss and Borsig. Records show previous users of 60cm gauge locomotives in Egypt included the Daira Khasa de SA, Le Khedive (a sugar company) and the Cairo Drainage Works[4]. All locomotives traced were coal burners, coal being regularly imported for the use of naval and military shipping.

Following the first (unsuccessful) Turkish assault, construction of a 2ft 6in gauge line from Port Said to Mohamedieh (near Romani) was put in hand in January 1916. It was decided to use Royal Engineers construction companies to build this line. On March 8th 1916 a unit War Diary records "petrol locomotives on 2ft 6in gauge lines east of Canal very troublesome, especially the gears". By May 19th the railhead had reached the 41km mark. Hawthorn Leslie 55hp petrol locos, ROD nos. 61 -83, works nos. 3107-29, are known to have been employed on this system.

There are few published references to the construction or operation of the 60cm gauge railways, but they were evidently being worked hard. A War Diary for July 5th records: "Went to Shallufa and Kubri to inspect Decauville[5] - the engines were worn out;" and on July 6th:" Advised scrapping Decauville from Quarantine Post to Ain Musa and extending 2ft 6in line which already goes from Shatt to Quarantine Post."

The Second Turkish Attack

In June 1916 a second Turkish Expeditionary Force, comprising some 16,000 men, reinforced by German and Austrian machine gun, mortar and artillery companies, was assembling on the Sinai-Palestine frontier. The Turks attacked on 4th August 1916, but the defending British and ANZAC

107. The 60cm gauge system extended out into the desert, for the supply of the defending troops. With no ready supply of ballast material available, the line is simply laid flat on the sand. An unidentified 30hp Koppel 0-4-0WT is pictured here with a train of track panels, used in constructing the line. (Australian War Memorial, G1460)

106. This 60cm gauge railway connected with the 2ft 6in gauge line at Serepeum East and, like that in the preceding illustration, extended out towards the front line. Motive power is again an Orenstein & Koppel 0-4-0WT, this time the 20hp version. (Australian War Memorial G4764)

107. Men of the 5th Suffolk Regiment, returning from a bathe in the Suez Canal, hitch a lift on a 2ft 6in gauge train conveying 'tibbin' (camel food), in the summer of 1916. The locomotive is one of a batch of 12 Avonside 60hp petrol locomotives fitted with Parsons 4-cylinder engines. The War Office orders to Avonside and Hawthorn Leslie were both builders' first significant orders for internal combustion locomotives. (Rogers)

108. Beersheba station on 1st November 1917, after its capture by the 4th Australian Light Horse Brigade. One of the station buildings has suffered minor damage to its roof, but a Turkish 1050mm gauge locomotive (right) appears to have escaped unscathed.
(Imperial War Museum, Q13165)

troops stationed at Romani and on Wellington Ridge held firm and defeated the attack, taking 4,000 prisoners. The Turks retreated back into Palestine; the Suez Canal was no longer threatened, and from now on British and Dominion forces would be on the offensive.

The Empire Strikes Back

In early 1917 the Turkish lines covered 25 miles from the Mediterranean coastline along natural ridges to Tel-es-Sheria, and thence to Beersheba, which guarded the last water supplies before the desert proper. Close to the coast was Gaza, which commanded the old coast road, and was regarded as the 'portcullis' to Palestine and the natural focus of any attack. The first British offensive took place on 25th March 1917, when units of British infantry, supported by ANZAC cavalry, penetrated the outskirts of Gaza, before being forced to withdraw. A second attack on 17th–19th April, despite being reinforced with the added weight of eight Mark 1 tanks, was also unsuccessful. A new commander, General Sir Edmund Allenby, realised further attacks on Gaza would be futile, and instead conceived a strategy to take Beersheba, and drive east and north east from there. A massive build up began in preparation for the attack.

Most of the railway construction during this phase was of course on the standard gauge. But 2ft 6in and 60cm gauge equipment that was no longer needed in the Suez zone was recovered and used to help the build up of men and material. A 2ft 6in gauge line was commenced from Deir-el-Balah on the coast towards Shellal, near Gamli. The railway ran along the south side of the Wadi Ghuzze (Wadi Ghazzee or Wadi Gaza) valley for 19km, later extended by another 4km Contemporary sources record that the line was within range of Turkish artillery but was not significantly troubled by enemy action. It is not clear if the line had reached Shellal by the time Beersheba fell on 31st October, but it is recorded as having enabled large reserves of supplies and ammunition to be brought up near to the front line. Meanwhile a standard gauge line from Shellal had reached Gamli, and from here construction of a 60cm gauge line was put in hand on 30th July 1917. The crossing of the Wadi Ghuzze was a formidable challenge, with grades of 1 in 35, and the maximum load permitted on the 25lb/30lb track was 12 tons nett!

Triumph at Beersheba

On 31st October 1917 the attack came at last, involving elements of the British 20th Corps, the ANZAC Mounted Division, Australian Mounted Division, and Imperial Camel Corps troops. The Australian 4th Light Horse Brigade finally took Beersheba in the late evening after a spirited attack during which they sustained 200 casualties but took 11,500 Turkish prisoners. Such was the speed of the attack that the Turks were unable to destroy the vital water supplies. The Turks retreated and by November were pushed back as far as Tel-es-Sheria. Allenby's forces entered Jerusalem on 7th December 1917 and the campaign culminated in the fall of Damascus on 1st October 1918.[6]

The Palestine-Arabia campaign was primarily a war of movement, with mounted troops used in their 'classic' role, and in complete contrast to the artillery war being waged on the Western Front. But phases of both defence and attack were presaged by a carefully thought out and skillfully implemented supply and logistic build up, ensuring that the fighting men were able to fulfil their role efficiently. This unglamorous function is often ignored by the history books, but was no less vital to the men on the ground. It is sad, therefore, that the one known physical relic of the narrow gauge railways used in the Palestine campaign, an Orenstein and Koppel 0-4-2WT numbered 'Re5', which was shipped back to Australia at the end of the war and put on display in Melbourne, was removed and scrapped in the late 1930's.[7]

[1] *The Light Horse regiments were mounted infantry. Although they trained with sword and lance, in battle they were equipped with rifle and bayonet only, and generally fought dismounted. Nevertheless their horses gave them useful mobility – whether ordered to attack or to retreat.*

[2] *"Another look at the Suez Canal Railways of World War 1" by Paul Cotterell, Harakavet 19:10.*

[3] *By John K Browning, Ray Ellis and Hugh Hughes, published in Industrial Railway Record 141; supplemented by notes in Harakavet, the journal of the Middle East Railway Study Group, by Hugh Hughes and Paul Cotterell.*

[4] *Research by Hugh Hughes, Industrial Railway Record 141.*

[5] *"Decauville" was the generic title used by the British military to refer to railways of 60cm gauge; it does not imply that material built by Decauville was in use.*

[6] *Light railways of (mainly) 2ft 6in gauge were in use in later stages of the Palestine campaign; notes appear in Harakavet 14 and 17.*

[7] *A Military Mystery Tour, John Browning (Industrial Railway Record 141).*

Chapter Nine

SWORDS INTO PLOUGHSHARES

Disposals of WDLR equipment after 1919.

ONCE HOSTILITIES CEASED THERE BEGAN THE HUGE TASK of reconstruction. In the short term this meant an actual increase in light railway working as large numbers of refugees and their belongings were ferried home, and materials brought in to begin the work of rebuilding shattered towns and villages. In the other direction unused military stores and ammunition were worked back to main line railheads.

During 1919 the Light Railway Operating Companies were gradually sent home and the lines handed over to the French and Belgian authorities. The French continued to employ the light railways on reconstruction work for several years, even running public passenger services in some cases, but most such usage ended by 1926. Most of the 60cm gauge lines were then lifted, but isolated sections were retained for industrial use, notably as feeder systems for transporting sugar beet from field to sugar refinery, but occasionally also by other industries, such as the cement factory at Haubourdin.

The Ministry of Munitions

Throughout the war most military supplies, including railway plant, were ordered by the Ministry of Munitions (MoM), who now set up a Disposals Board to sell off this huge mass of surplus material. The current contracts for batches of 20hp and 40hp Simplex petrol tractors were immediately terminated, but not, for whatever reason, an order placed with the Hunslet Engine Co. in January 1918 for 80 more 4-6-0T's for the Italian and Palestine fronts. Building steam locomotives was a much slower business than the 'assembly line' production of petrol tractors, and by Armistice Day only 16 had been delivered, 14 to Italy and 2 to Palestine. So during the early months of 1919 Hunslets quietly continued with this order, the now unwanted locomotives simply piling up at Purfleet Wharf, Essex, the intended shipping point.

109. Best known of all the WDLR disposals in Britain was the sale of six Baldwin 4-6-0T's for the newly opened Ashover Light Railway. HUMMY, BLW 45227/17, previously WDLR No. 645, poses at Ashover (Butts) with two of the railway's Gloucester Railway & Wagon Co., coaches, which, although newly built, utilised second-hand bogies from a WDLR 'D' class wagon. (Author's collection)

110. Many ex-WDLR Motor Rails not only gave long service on British industrial lines, but remained in remarkably original condition. One such was 40hp MR461 (LR2182) of 1917, seen out of use at the Furness Brick and Tile Co., Askham, in 1963, where it had been replaced by a more modern Simplex diesel. The loco survives today at Beverley Army Museum.
(courtesy H D Bowtell)

Two new Hunslets were actually found a home with the Royal Engineers at Gosport[1] and then authority eventually woke up. Orders were issued that (a) the final 20 should be built to 2ft 6in gauge in the hope that this would make them more saleable; and (b) Hunslets were directed to retain these locomotives on completion and to make every effort to find customers for them. Fortunately this proved successful. One loco (Hunslet 1356) was immediately purchased by Jee's Hartshill Granite Quarries and completed to their 2ft 6½in gauge, the other 19 steadily found homes from August 1919 onwards.

An important part of the Disposal Board's efforts was the magazine "Surplus." Published fortnightly by the Board from June 1919 onwards each issue carried details of all surplus war material up for disposal - from complete chemical factories to piles of worn out army boots. A railway materials section was included in every issue, with the locomotive dump at Purfleet first featuring in issue No. 5 dated 1st August 1919. At its largest this dump apparently approached 300 locomotives, not only brand new Hunslet 4-6-0T, Simplexes of both sizes, and a handful of Hudswell Clarke 0-6-0WT that never made it to Italy, but also 21 Baldwin 4-6-0T and 3 Alco 2-6-2T that had been shipped back during 1918 for rebuilding by W G Bagnall Ltd. at Stafford to ease pressure on the front line workshops in France.

Being either brand new or newly overhauled and no doubt available at somewhat less than their cost the Purfleet locomotives proved reasonably easy to sell. This was particularly so for the Motor Rails, for arduous war service had proved the soundness of the design and the usefulness of 60cm gauge temporary light railways in general. Many went to civil engineering contractors and quarrying companies, and others to agricultural and forestry lines, the latter being primarily overseas. The steam locomotives proved more difficult to sell but all are thought to have eventually found new homes. Four of the Baldwins rebuilt by Bagnall were among the eleven of this type that definitely saw service in Britain, the other seven possibly coming from Baldwins that had been shipped back to Purfleet but never actually overhauled.

Locomotives on active service

The main problem was disposing of all the locomotives still on 'active service.' Surviving Ministry records are of course non-existent but from a careful analysis of sales adverts in "Surplus" and technical journals such as 'The Engineer' and 'Machinery Market,' together with numerous scraps of information derived from a great variety of other sources a general picture can be built up.

During the summer of 1919 a number of redundant 60cm gauge locomotives (presumably from France) were shipped back to the important wartime port of Richborough in Kent. A two day auction sale there in November 1919 included a dozen each of either type of Simplex, a further dozen petrol-electric locos, and six Baldwin 4-6-0T. Like many another "Ministry Auction" before and since, it was not an unqualified success, with many lots failing to sell, and it was not until the following September that the exercise was repeated. This time the auctioneers advertised "74 petrol and petrol electric tractors 40 or 45hp 2ft gauge," implying no further importation of 20hp Simplexes. The following March auctioneers Fuller Horsey were having their third try on behalf of the MoM with 44 petrol electrics and 24 40hp Simplexes on offer. This rather suggests that only six internal combustion locos had sold at the previous auction. Ominously all three auctions included "six Baldwin 4-6-0T," no doubt the same unhappy lot. With rebuilt examples available at Purfleet, or better still brand new Hunslets, it is little wonder that no-one got terribly excited.

With the need to clear the Richborough and Purfleet sites and return them to civilian use, unsold locomotives and other plant were moved to sundry other Government depots to be included in various smaller auctions or sold by Private treaty. In June 1923 all remaining war surplus material was handed over to the specially created George Cohen & Armstrong Disposal Corporation who handled all remaining UK sales. These included that pair of Baldwin 4-6-0T that ultimately became BRIDGET and GUY on the Ashover Light Railway, whose unusually narrow (for a common carrier) gauge was chosen largely because of the availability of cheap surplus WDLR equipment.

111. Hunslet 4-6-0T No. 1218, ex WDLR 306, was one of a number of this type which made successful new careers on sugar cane railways in Australia. HE1218 was rebuilt by Hunslets in 1924, before being shipped to Gin Gin mill, 30 miles west of Bundaberg, Queensland, where she worked until the early 1960's. The prominent extended smokebox was a much later local modification. (J W Knowles)

112. Perhaps the most exotic fate of all was enjoyed by a number of protected Simplexes which migrated to the remote Tokar-Trinkitat Light Railway in the Sudan. Here some steel plate was removed to improve crew comfort, but WDLR number plates continued to be displayed. WDLR 2190 hauls a train of cotton bales, sometime in the 1920's.
(courtesy Dave Ellis)

The poor results at Richborough and Purfleet meant that many locomotives and much other equipment was sold directly 'on site' where it lay in France. Some locos were bought by Continental dealers but many of the British built machines were purchased by UK firms. Robert Hudson Ltd.were particularly active in purchasing wagons and trackwork, often of their own manufacture, as well as "Hudson" 0-6-0WT which were returned to their builders Hudswell Clarke for reconditioning before resale. Motor Rail operated similarly with their own products, often acting in conjunction with other interested firms.

One other active participant was Messrs Honeywill Bros., with offices in London and a works (The Kent Construction and Engineering Co. Ltd.) at Ashford, Kent. Much to the annoyance of Motor Rail they built up a thriving business in buying up cheaply and then rebuilding many ex-WDLR Simplexes, marketing them as "Planet Simplexes." This work included much ingenious rebuilding including using 40hp Simplex underframes as a basis for standard gauge locos, or incorporating second hand Motor Rail parts in otherwise 'new' machines. They also dealt in other WDLR plant such as Hunslet 4-6-0T, 'D' class bogie wagons and much trackwork. The business ceased trading in 1927 but was re-formed as F C Hibberd & Co. Ltd., who built the 'Planet' range of petrol and diesel locomotives until 1964.

Other Combatants' Locomotives

Apart from all the British 60cm gauge stock there were also large stocks from the French, German and US Armies. Generally the MoM did not concern itself with this, although a quantity of captured German Deutz petrol/paraffin locos were advertised in the autumn of 1919. Their fate is unknown though it has been suggested that at least two came to Britain, one to a south Humberside brickworks and another purchased by Hudswell Clarke for evaluation and ideas for their projected range of small petrol locomotives.

No such inhibitions were shown by British dealers. Honeywill Bros. in particular handled a number of French locomotives, particularly the 50hp 0-4-0 Baldwin 'gas mechnicals.' At least two were sold in Britain, one surviving as the Festiniog Railways's MOELWYN, albeit much rebuilt. However most British companies simply sold the plant 'ex site' within France, R H Neal Ltd. once advertising 150 Baldwin petrol locos as being available, although only one definitely returned to their London plant depot.

In general most of the US Army equipment was either handed over to the French authorities or shipped home, but there were some interesting exceptions. The most notable was the sale of three Baldwin 2-6-2T to Penrhyn Quarries in 1923. They were a sad failure on the main line there but one was subsequently resold to Queensland, Australia in 1940. Here it proved its worth, putting in many years hard work at Fairymead sugar mill before being preserved.

With nearly 2,500 having been built it is unsurprising that the German Army 'Feldbahn' 0-8-0T should find a ready sale throughout the world. Inevitably the fate of only a small proportion is known but many put in 50 odd years' service in countries as diverse as France, Poland, Turkey and Mozambique, and a number are preserved.

Compiling a complete and accurate record of the fate of all the 60cm gauge locomotives employed in World War 1 will probably never be completely possible. Nevertheless attempting it is a fascinating task which it is hoped these notes will encourage.[2] What can be said, however, is that the majority of such locomotives did survive the hostilities, even if their subsequent career was brief and, in many cases, will ever be shrouded in mystery.

[1] see "Steam and Sail to Gilkicker Point" by K Taylorson, "The Narrow Gauge 133," winter 1991/2.
[2] it is the intention to publish a list of all known WDLR locomotive disposals in a future publication. All contributions (preferably quoting sources) will be welcomed by the author, and should be sent to the address on page 1.

113. Longest-lived of all ex-WDLR locomotives were the Baldwin 4-6-0T's supplied to sugar cane tramways in India. Helped by a short working 'season' each year, and the Indian talent for making repairs, several examples worked on into the 1990's. Motipur No. 2, BLW45231/17 (ex WDLR 1099) is seen here on 25th February 1984. (L G Marshall)

APPENDIX 1

MOVING ARTILLERY ON THE LIGHT RAILWAYS

While the transport of artillery pieces by light railways was not envisaged even by the most enthusiastic proponent of the 60cm gauge concept, it did not take the British Army long to realise that this could be a valuable function. Guns - and their ammunition - could be moved far more efficiently on rails than they could be dragged by horses along muddy roads. They could also be spirited away more quickly if gunners were threatened by an enemy advance. Within a short time of the light railways' "official" recognition, various experiments were tried to determine the best type of gun wagons. Favourite soon became the standard 'F' class well wagon, with its stanchions removed and steel troughs slung either side, supported by girders or beams across the body.

At the loading point, the modified wagon is backed into a position with road access, and detachable ramps put in place either side (illus. 114). The troughs are then positioned (illus. 115) and the gun, barrel first, manoeuvred by soldiers - or more likely chain-hauled by the locomotive - up the ramp until it is in position (illus. 116), with the tail spade projecting over one bogie. It will be noted that the wheel troughs here only extend about three-quarters of the way along the wagon, this is because the gun barrel projects over the remainder. The loading ramps are then dismantled and stowed on the wagon body alongside the gun, for use when unloading it. The final action (not illustrated) is to run the gun's limber up on to the wagon, resting on the gun tail or, if the gun is too large or too high-tailed, the limber will be carried on a separate wagon.

114

115

The fourth and fifth illustrations depict the same operation, featuring an even larger calibre gun, taking place in rather more realistic conditions in the field. The ramp here is in four parts, supported on a 'cradle' of sleepers. Illus. 117 shows the cable being **116**

117

used to pull the gun up the ramp by the locomotive, British Westinghouse PE No. 2005 (the wagon is of course braked and chocked to stop it from moving during this operation). Illus. 118 shows the gun secured and ready for departure, though before doing so the crew will probably insert a specially long coupling bar between the locomotive and the wagon, due to the overhang provided by the gun barrel.

(All illustrations – Museum of Army Transport)

118

APPENDIX 2

THE WORKSHOP TRAIN

From "The Locomotive" Magazine, October 15, 1918

The vehicles shown in the accompanying illustrations form part of the units of a series of workshop trains built by the Gloucester Railway Carriage and Wagon Co. to the order of the Ministry of Munitions for service overseas.

The increased mobility of a train of this description and corresponding advantages over a workshop proper will be appreciated when the accuracy of modern artillery fire is considered. An ordinary workshop is quickly "spotted" by the enemy air force, its position registered, and there is consequently every possibility that the whole establishment will be quickly wiped out by shell fire. Compared with which, the mobile workshop illustrated may be frequently moved from point to point, so that the destruction by enemy gun fire is rendered far more difficult.

The vehicles are constructed to run on the 60cm (1ft 11in) gauge military railway, which is that adopted for the light railways in France acting as feeder lines from the standard gauge main lines. As such the underframes, bogies etc., are practically standard with the rolling stock in service. The underframes are constructed of timber, well braced by angle trussing. The bogies are similarly wood

119. An excellent side on view of the generator car. (Museum of Army Transport)

120. Machinery Car No. 2, showing the lathe (centre). Note also the handbrake and miniscule platform for the brakesman. (Museum of Army Transport)

framed, with the drawbars built in, and the pull transmitted through the bogies - a reversal of the usual broad gauge practice of arranging the bogies, and taking the drawbar pull through the headstocks of the vehicles.

The running gear consists of cast steel wheels, and oil axle boxes, each vehicle is fitted with a hand brake at one end, the bogie at this end being extended, so as to form a platform for the operator to stand on. The bodies are arranged to that the side doors open out in two portions, the top halves forming canopies and the lower halves acting as the working platform for the mechanics. Storm curtains are also provided so that in bad weather the men can be protected from the elements.

Each train consists of six vehicles, with an overall length of 123ft, the particular vehicles being - generating car (1), machinery cars (2), tool van (1), stores van (1) and officers' car (1).

The Generator Car, shown in illus. 119, is perhaps the most interesting vehicle. The equipment consists of two Aster petrol engines, arranged at each end of the vehicle, which are direct coupled to 10 kilowatt dynamos - the hp of the engines being 15/20. An air compressor by Messrs. Reavell, of Ipswich, driven by 10hp motor, is arranged in the centre of the car, the reservoir for which may be noticed as being slung from the roof of the vehicle. Water and petrol tanks are arranged underneath the underframe in a convenient manner. The electrical switches etc. are conveniently arranged as may be seen by reference to the illustration.

It will be understood that there is a considerable weight carried in this car, and in working condition the underframe is blocked up to the centre, to relieve the loading, and also to steady the vehicle when the machinery is at work, similar arrangements being provided at the four corners of the underframe. The principal dimensions of this vehicle are - length over body 17ft 8in, width over body 5ft 4in, centre of bogies 13ft 9in, height from rail to top of body 9ft 1in, weight, 8 tons, 9cwt, 3qrs.

121. Half of the complete train, with (from left): Tool Van, Machinery Car, Machinery Car No. 2.
(Museum of Army Transport)

A Machinery Car. The equipment of this car consists of:- one duplex emery grinder, one 30-in grindstone, one rapid hack-saw, one 1in vertical drilling machine. The first two machines are connected to an overhead shafting which is driven by a 3hp motor, the other two machines being driven direct. The principal dimensions of this vehicle are the same as the generator car. The weight is 4 tons 19 cwt 3 qrs.

The Second Machinery Car is shown in illus. 120 and has a very useful equipment consisting of:- one 8in shaping machine one 6in lathe and a small drilling machine, the arrangement of the drive being somewhat similar to the first car, with the exception that the motor for the lathe is attached to the bottom portion of the drop door, and connected by driving belt to the overhead shafting.

The Tool Van arranged next in order to the machinery cars is provided with fitter's benches, and vices, with the usual arrangement of drawers, shelves etc., for the men to store their light tools when not in use.

The Stores Van is provided with two light jib cranes, one on either side, so as to swing clear for raising or lowering any heavy equipment, and is provided with rows of shelves, and bins for the storage of miscellaneous equipment, the floor space being used for storing the smith's hearths, anvils, jacks etc. The usual range of pneumatic tools is carried, and the portable hearths have direct driven fans, the power being supplied by a cable from the main electric circuit.

The Officers' Car forming the rear of the train is partitioned off so as to make two offices, one is a small private office, and the main portion being a general office for the use of the staff in charge of the train. Suitable arrangements are made for heating either by means of a portable radiator or a small coal-fired stove, and facilities for office use, such as pigeon holes, cupboards etc. are conveniently arranged. The lighting of this vehicle as well as the whole train is electric, both portable and fixed lights being freely supplied, the cables for the various circuits being arranged with flexible couplings between each vehicle.

The whole train forms a very interesting development of workshop practice as required by the conditions under which it works, and there is no doubt that the usefulness of such a portable plant is without question. Furthermore, the arrangement of such a variety of useful equipment on the narrow gauge of 60cm provides an illustration of the possibilities with careful design for the general usefulness of a narrow gauge railway for services of this description.

122. An end on view of the complete train. Note the wooden stanchions to support the working platform. Power is here being taken from adjoining buildings, though in the 'field' would be supplied by the generator car.
(Museum of Army Transport)

APPENDIX 3

GENERAL TRAFFIC-OPERATIONAL REGULATIONS

Brakesmen are in sole charge of their trucks under officers or NCO's of their own unit. This officer or NCO will travel in the rear truck of each train or section of train. These will wear white armlets and will be empowered to ask for any assistance required in case of breakdown or other emergency.

Passengers - No-one is permitted the use of trucks on the outward journey except brakesmen, RAMC on duty on the train, and officers or NCO's or their representatives actually in charge of stores.

Smoking - No smoking is permissible further from Bois de Bray than a point 400 yards west of the Bethune Road for trains going to 'Liverpool', 'Birmingham', 'Leeds,' and no further from Maroeuil than 'Artillery Corner' in the case of trains leaving Maroeuil.

DUTIES OF OFFICER i/c TRAIN

The officer will be distinguished by the wearing of a white armlet.

He will supervise in the office the booking in writing of all the trucks required by units, and the keeping of a record of all traffic.

He will supervise the loading of all trucks allocated to units, and see that each truck is properly, safely and sufficiently loaded.

He is responsible that all orders in connection with the traffic are duly observed.

He will himself travel in rear truck of his train, and will be in charge of it, or will detail a responsible NCO to take his place.

DUTIES OF NCO i/c TRAIN

Before the train starts he will check the total number of his trucks, and also the particular number of each truck, together with the names of the brakesmen travelling on each truck.

He is responsible that brakesmen know their destination, understand their duties, and carry them out.

Each responsible NCO will travel in the rear truck of his train or section of train. He will carry with him the necessary tools for urgent repairs, and will at once go to the cause of any trouble.

He must take charge in the absence of superior authority.

Outgoing - He will report to each patrol or pointsman on duty as the last truck of his train passes.

Incoming - No truck must return from 'Liverpool' or 'Birmingham' until the whole of the train has passed 'Sniper's Corner' on the outward journey. On his return he will immediately report at the office the time of his arrival, and whether or not any irregularity has occurred.

DUTIES OF BRAKESMEN

In the absence of an officer or NCO of his own unit, the front brakesman is in charge of his truck.

As the safety of the train largely depends on the individual brakesman, each must learn and act with initiative.

The brakesman is responsible for the proper braking of the truck, for its safe arrival at its destination, which he must know, and that all orders concerning traffic are duly obeyed.

Any mishap, irregularity, failure to deliver stores etc., must be reported at once by the brakesman to the Officer or NCO of his own unit in charge of the train, in the absence of whom he will report direct to the office by telephone or word of mouth.

The brakesman has authority to ask for assistance from anyone on the train in case of emergency.

Extract from "General Traffic-Operational Regulations" 8th April 1916

E D Galbraith (Capt)
for Brig-General
DA & QMG, XVII Corps

APPENDIX 4

CROSSING OF 60cm OVER BROAD AND METRE GAUGE RAILWAYS

DLR's Circular 1598.C.18 of 19th July 1918.

(1) All crossings of 60cm over Broad or Metre Gauge fall under one of the following headings:-

A.	Mechanically	protected.	Controlled	by R.O.D.
B.	do	do	do	by L.R.
C.	Not	do	do	Manned by R.O.D.
D.	Not	do	do	do by L.R.
E.	Neither mechanically protected or manned.			

(2) In the case of A. and B, the crossing is protected by fixed signals, and trains are only allowed to pass over the crossing by permission of the Blockman in charge of the Mechanical signalling.

(3) In the case of C. and D., the crossing is protected by Warning Boards (Stop, or Whistle as the case may be) and no train, except trains of the Gauge which have preference, will pass over the crossing without first receiving the "all right" signal from the Flagman.

(4) In the case of E., no trains, except trains of the Gauge which have preference, must proceed on to the crossing, without first stopping and ascertaining that the road is clear. On the train coming to a stand clear of the crossing, the Guard will proceed to the crossing, and having satisfied himself that the road is clear, flag his train across.

(5) The class under which each crossing is to be protected, also the Gauge whose trains are to have preference, will be decided upon between ROD and the ADLR concerned, and the necessary instructions issued to the staff accordingly.

Page 112-113: A superb 1920 advertisement from Baldwins, featuring standard and narrow gauge locomotives (and a naval gun for good measure) supplied to four Allied governments. The stunning total of 5528 locomotives (exceeding the total supplied by all other manufacturers combined) will be noted. (courtesy Railway Gazette)

Page 114: A 1920 advert from Motor Rail, featuring the classic view of Vimy Ridge, and a line-up of armoured Simplexes. (courtesy Railway Gazette)

Page 115: Hunslets advertised their surplus ex-WDLR 4-6-0T's extensively. This 1920 advert features "SPENCER" which was allocated WDLR number 3224, but never served with the WDLR, going into store at Barnbow Depot, Leeds. From here it went to the Harrogate Gas Works, where it worked until 1943. (courtesy Railway Gazette)

Page 116: Despite the relative lack of success of the Baguley petrol-mechanical locomotives, McEwan Pratt were happy to feature an example in their adverts. The locomotive illustrated is the 20hp version, supplied in 1919 for forestry work. (courtesy Railway Gazette)

BALDWIN

War Activities

DEPENDABILITY was placed on BALDWIN locomotives of all types by the Allied Governments for the transportation of men, supplies and ordnance on the various battle fronts. These governments not only ordered these locomotives in quantity but rightfully demanded that they should be completed in the shortest possible time.

Ten-Wheeled Six-Coupled Tank Locomotive for the British Government
Gauge, 1'-11⅝"; Cylinders, 9" x 12"; Driving-wheels, diam., 23½"
Weight, total, 32,500 pounds.

Pechot Type Locomotive for the French Government
Gauge, 1'-11⅝"; Cylinders, 6.89" x 9.45"; Driving-wheels, diam., 25.59";
Weight, total, 28,200 pounds.

BRITISH GOVERNMENT:—The Director-General of Movements and Transportation utilized one thousand BALDWIN locomotives for transportation on the Belgian, French, Macedonian, Egyptian and Mesopotamian fronts, composed of the following:

495 TEN-WHEELED, six-coupled, side-tank locomotives specified on pages 31, 114 and 122 of this issue; illustrated on pages 53, 58, 62, 73, 74, 78 and 81 of the pictorial section.

70 FOUR-COUPLED, saddle-tank locomotives of standard gauge for shunting service.

50 SIX-COUPLED, saddle-tank locomotives of standard gauge for heavy shunting service.

75 SIX-COUPLED, double-ender, saddle-tank locomotives of standard gauge illustrated on pages 87 and 89 of this issue.

150 "CONSOLIDATION" type locomotives of standard gauge for main-line freight service, illustrated below.

40 "MALLET" type locomotives of meter gauge for heavy freight service, specified on page 132.

FRENCH GOVERNMENT:—Twelve hundred and fifty-eight BALDWIN locomotives of various types were supplied to the War Department and Government Railways composed of the following:

600 GASOLINE locomotives of 60 cm. gauge for trench service.

8 FOUR-COUPLED, fireless locomotives for powder factory service.

30 SIX-COUPLED, saddle-tank locomotives of 60 cm. gauge for shunting service. Twenty of these were built and shipped 18 days after the order was placed.

280 "PECHOT" type locomotives of 60 cm. gauge for use in the advanced areas, as illustrated.

50 SIX-COUPLED, side-tank locomotives of meter gauge for general service.

290 "MIKADO" type locomotives of 4'-9" gauge for the Paris, Lyons & Mediterranean and Nord Railways.

Record No. 93 in English or French, describing BALDWIN War Industries, will be forwarded upon request. Catalogs of BALDWIN railway and industrial locomotives—steam, internal combustion or electric—can be had at any time.

THE BALDWIN LOCOMOTIVE WORKS

PHILADELPHIA, PA., U. S. A.

Consolidation Type Locomotive for the British Government
Gauge, 4'-8½"; Cylinders, 21" x 28"; Driving-wheels, diam., 56"; Weight, total Engine, 162,510 pounds.

LOCOMOTIVES

On All War Fronts

General Joffre has said: "This is a railway war. The battle of the Marne was won by the railways of France." According to Sir Guy Granet, if it had not been for the prompt and efficient deliveries of BALDWIN locomotives, some of the accomplishments of the British Army would not have been possible.

RUSSIAN GOVERNMENT:—During the earlier part of the war the Russian War Office, due to the great distances to be covered, placed orders for 923 BALDWIN locomotives of various types.

350 GASOLINE locomotives of 75-centimeter gauge for trench service as illustrated.

8 FOUR-COUPLED side-tank locomotives of narrow gauge for general service.

525 "DECAPOD" type locomotives of 5' gauge for heavy freight service.

40 "MALLET" type locomotives of 3'-6" gauge for freight service on the Vologda-Archangel Railway.

UNITED STATES GOVERNMENT:—While "carrying on" the contracts with our Allies we also supplied our own forces in France with 2,367 BALDWIN locomotives of various types.

186 GASOLINE locomotives of 60 cm. gauge for trench service.

20 GASOLINE locomotives of standard gauge for advanced areas.

195 SIX-COUPLED, double-ender, side-tank locomotives of 60 cm. gauge.

1966 "CONSOLIDATION" type locomotives for freight service over American transportation lines in France.

11 FOURTEEN-INCH railway gun mounts illustrated on page 57.

2 IMPROVED FOURTEEN-INCH railway gun mounts illustrated below.

38 SEVEN-INCH caterpillar gun mounts.

SUMMARY of BALDWIN locomotives supplied to the Allied Governments during the war:

Broad Gauge Steam,	3246	Broad Gauge Gasoline,	20
Narrow " "	1146	Narrow " "	1136

Total, 5548 locomotives.

Gasoline Locomotive for the Russian Government
Gauge, 2'-5½"; Weight, 15,000 pounds

Six-Coupled Double-Ender Tank Locomotive for the British Government
Gauge, 4'-8½"; Cylinders, 17" x 24"; Driving-wheels, diam., 44"; Weight, total, 150,900 pounds

BALDWIN SERVICE is always at your immediate command through any of our foreign offices, agencies and traveling technical representatives. We build locomotives of all types, for any purpose and to any designs or specifications.

THE BALDWIN LOCOMOTIVE WORKS

PHILADELPHIA, PA., U. S. A.

Fourteen-Inch Improved Naval Gun on Railway Mount
Maximum firing elevation, 45 degrees. Maximum effective range, 30 miles.

SIMPLEX

WAR

The MOTOR RAIL & TRAM CAR Co., Ltd.

SIMPLEX WORKS,

BEDFORD, ENGLAND.

THE HUNSLET ENGINE Co., Ltd.,

LOCOMOTIVE BUILDERS,

LEEDS, ENGLAND.

Telephone:
20877 (3 lines).

Telegrams:
"ENGINE, LEEDS."

4-6-0 Side Tank Locomotive as built for service on British War Fronts—60 c/m. Gauge.

LOCOMOTIVES to suit

ANY GAUGE and EVERY CLASS OF SERVICE.

Works:—
THE HUNSLET ENGINE WORKS,
LEEDS.

London Office:—
1, BROAD STREET PLACE, E.C.
Telegrams:—"JIMCROW, LONDON."
Telephone:—7985 London Wall (2 lines).

Front End and Side Elevations of one of the above engines after conversion for home service.